African American Decision Makers in Healthcare:

Exploring the Impact of Mentoring on Professional Advancement

Deon L. Wolliston

DISSERTATION.COM

Boca Raton

African American Decision Makers in Healthcare:
Exploring the Impact of Mentoring on Professional Advancement

Dissertation.com
Boca Raton, Florida
USA • 2008

ISBN-10: 1-59942-655-2
ISBN-13: 978-1-59942-655-6

AFRICAN AMERICAN DECISION MAKERS IN HEALTHCARE: EXPLORING THE IMPACT OF MENTORING ON PROFESSIONAL ADVANCEMENT

Deon Lorraine Wolliston

A Dissertation Presented in Partial Fulfillment

of the Requirements for the Degree

Doctor of Health Administration

UNIVERSITY OF PHOENIX

August 2007

ABSTRACT

This qualitative case study explored the impact of mentoring on professional advancement among African American healthcare professionals. A nonrandom purposeful sample was used to identify 21 African American hospital decision makers employed in the specialty areas of nursing, medicine, pharmacy, and administration. Two central research questions were used to explore the role of mentoring on professional advancement and the participants' perception of the importance of mentorship and empowerment on their professional advancement. Data was analyzed using Moustakas (1994) modified van Kaam method of analysis. Results of the study showed that mentoring plays an important role in the professional advancement of African American hospital professionals. Additionally, the study participants believed that mentoring empowers African Americans for professional advancement.

TABLE OF CONTENTS

LIST OF TABLES

LIST OF FIGURES

CHAPTER 1: INTRODUCTION

The ethnically and racially diverse patient population that is being served in healthcare organizations has increased the need for diversity among patient care providers, including employees at the executive level of the organization (Gonzalez-Figueroa & Young, 2005). Diversity at the highest level of the hospital will raise the expectation and accountability of the executive team to be more diverse, therefore becoming more representative of the population that is being served. Voges predicted that "organizations that adopt inclusion are creating a competitive business advantage for themselves and they're going to continue to increase their population, their market share, and their revenue" (2006, p. 12).

According to the U.S. Department of Labor (2006), 1 in 3 Americans will be African American, Hispanic, Native American, or Asian/Pacific Islander by the year 2050. These changes in the United States will affect the communities that are being served. In order to show the value of diversity, healthcare professionals must reflect the communities in which service is being provided; therefore, diversity is needed at each level of the organization. Consequently, hospitals must also ensure that patients "have an increased comfort level doing business where you know that diversity is valued" (Voges, 2006, p. 12).

Evaluation of healthcare organizations revealed that minorities are underrepresented in healthcare leadership positions (Kelly, 2006; Larson, 2006; Voges, 2006). This imbalance becomes more evident at the highest level positions within the organization because the advancement of minorities above a director-level position to the top four or five levels of a hospital remains a challenge (Kelly, 2006; Larson, 2006; Voges, 2006).

Creating a diverse team of healthcare professionals requires career guidance and resources that empower minorities for advancement. Mid-career guidance or mentoring by a more experienced individual can prove beneficial in providing support to help expedite career advancement to the executive level (Voges, 2006). As African Americans continue to advance in healthcare management, the need for career support increases. However, the level of support needed for empowerment is not readily available (Voges, 2006).

Mentoring is considered to be an important attribute for empowerment. Junior medical faculty who were mentored displayed better preparation and skills than those who were not mentored (Koopman & Thiedke, 2005). Therefore, the impact of mentoring minority healthcare employees in preparation for executive-level positions may be beneficial and, indeed, necessary for expediting the number of years needed to achieve their career goals (McGlowan-Fellows & Thomas, 2005; Voges, 2006).

In a 2005 report on career advancement for minority healthcare professionals, senior minority executives agreed that minority students are not aware of the opportunities available to them (Gonzalez-Figueroa & Young, 2005). Career guidance through mentoring can be valuable during the early years of a fledgling professional's career, creating a positive mentoring relationship to reduce the risk of mid-career setbacks. The timing of a mentoring relationship is important because, in many situations, the opportunity for mentoring dwindles as individuals become tenured (Gonzalez-Figueroa & Young, 2005; Larson, 2006). Minority executives also stated that the first five years of starting a career are the most competitive and falling behind early will result in a continuous career lag (Gonzalez-Figueroa & Young, 2005).

Lack of knowledge of available mentoring resources for African Americans may be a result of their limited access to influential people or networking opportunities within their organization, thereby limiting the possibilities of a successful career (McGlowan-Fellows & Thomas, 2005). African Americans reported that they would like to have a mentor who could help them with career development and career navigation (Heggins, 2004). This qualitative case study, which explored the lived experiences of African American healthcare professionals who were and were not mentored during their careers, provided a better understanding of the barriers that limited their progression to decision-making roles within their organizations.

In a study of 100 highly successful individuals, 77% reported that mentoring was "crucial to their achievement" (Shaffer, Tallarica, & Walsh, 2000, p. 33). It was also reported that there is a correlation between mentoring and career advancement of African American women working in a corporate environment who have been mentored or have had role models (McGlowan-Fellows & Thomas, 2005). This study helps to determine if the impact of empowerment though mentoring was also applicable to healthcare and specifically to African Americans healthcare professionals.

Background of the Problem

Despite the efforts made to encourage minorities to pursue careers in healthcare, the goal of increased diversity is still unmet (Gathers, 2003; Hellinghausen, 2000; Romano, 2004). Several reports have addressed the reasons why minority ethnic groups are underrepresented in healthcare. However, most of the analyses pertaining to the prevalence of minorities in healthcare have evaluated careers such as nursing, medicine, science, and dentistry independently but not collectively across multiple disciplines at the executive level (Ambrose, 2003; Gathers, 2003).

Minority healthcare professionals believe there is lack of promotion for minorities after they advance to middle-management positions within the organization (Gathers, 2003; Larson, 2006). This lack of promotion is often referred to as the *glass* or t*eflon ceiling*, which is an invisible barrier preventing qualified minority employees from being promoted to executive-level positions (Barrett, Cervero, & Johnson-Bailey, 2004; Larson, 2006; Voges, 2006). In other words, it is an obstacle at the upper level of the organization past which an individual is unable to advance professionally in spite of his or her experience or credentials (Gathers, 2003).

African Americans employed in healthcare also reported that there is a sense of unfairness and lack of support of upward mobility for minorities (Gathers, 2003). Identifying the tools to support the advancement of minorities, specifically African Americans, may help to improve career advancement and increase awareness of this problem. Compared to 32% of Caucasian females, only 14% of African American females are employed in upper-level management positions (Edmondson Bell & Nkomo, 2003).

Despite having similar credentials, African American females are held to higher expectations, have less decision-making power, and earn less than their Caucasian counterparts (Edmondson Bell & Nkomo, 2003). African American males also face career challenges that have contributed to the low number of African American males working in healthcare. Some efforts have been made to recruit African American males, but the process is slow and minorities overall continue to feel unrewarded for their hard work ("A Race Ethnicity Comparison," 2002).

In an effort to support minority healthcare professionals, organizations such as the National Council on Healthcare Leadership (NCHL) have developed initiatives to support the advancement of racial and ethnic minorities in senior management and leadership positions, and to provide educational support for cultural diversity in healthcare (*The Black Perspective Online*, 2000). These initiatives include diversity education programs that bring together midlevel to upper level healthcare leaders from various ethnic groups. These leaders will later serve as the change agents in their organizations.

Additional initiatives by the NCHL include mentoring programs designed to prepare healthcare managers to serve as mentors to junior managers in their organizations (*The Black Perspective Online*, 2000). Similar to the NCHL's diversity initiatives, hospital organizations are implementing diversity programs that are expected to improve the number of minority healthcare executives. These programs are intended to develop and prepare young executives to become future leaders of hospital organizations (Reilly, 2003).

Statement of the Problem

Despite the additional efforts of healthcare organizations to increase diversity among healthcare leaders, the number of minority executives in the healthcare industry has remained in the single digits (Hellinghausen, 2000). A larger number of Caucasian males and females have achieved executive-level positions such as chief executive officer, chief operating officer, and vice president in hospitals as compared to African Americans working in the same setting ("A Race Ethnicity Comparison," 2002). Career advancement of African American healthcare employees to executive levels has become more difficult after reaching a midlevel position in a hospital organization (Larson, 2006).

Minorities continue to face numerous obstacles in reaching the highest level of healthcare management. Two of these obstacles include "getting into the field young and having enough mid-career guidance and high-level continuing education to get to the executive-level position" (Gonzalez-Figueroa & Young, 2005, p. 8). Secondly, healthcare organizations have not completely addressed the need for diversity at the executive level (Larson, 2006).

Several healthcare organizations and colleges have embraced the concept of mentoring in an effort to recruit and retain minorities (Blancero & DelCampo, 2005; Gonzalez-Figueroa & Young, 2005; Larson, 2006; Ralston, 2003). In spite of the effort to empower minorities to advance to upper level positions, there appears to be a lack of sensitivity to the individual needs and necessary resources to support the professional growth of racial minorities in the healthcare industry (Ambrose, 2003). Therefore, the number of African American healthcare executives continues to be poorly represented with only 1-2% of healthcare executives being African Americans (Griffin, 2001; Hellinghausen, 2000; Woog, 2005).

This qualitative case study was designed to provide a better understanding of the career accomplishments of African American healthcare administrators and executives through exploration of their lived experiences as they relate to mentoring, as well as perceived difficulties in advancing to executive positions within their career fields. Professionals in the areas of medicine, nursing, pharmacy, and health administration were selected to participate in this study. Data were collected through tape recorded, open-ended interviews in order to solicit perceptions pertaining to career advancement and mentoring.

Purpose of the Study

The purpose of this qualitative case study was to provide a better understanding of the role of mentorship in advancing the careers of African American healthcare administrators and executives through exploration of their lived experiences as they relate to mentoring as well as perceived difficulties in advancing to executive positions within their careers. The participants of this study were African Americans healthcare professionals working in a medical inpatient facility in the southeastern United States who were on a career path that is conducive for advancement to a decision-making position. A nonrandom snowball method of sampling was used to select study participants for this qualitative case study. Data were collected using an open-ended question, semistructured interview process.

The questions focused on the role of mentoring in the participants' careers, and the perceived impact of mentoring on their professional development as well as perceived obstacles to advancement within their careers. A follow up discussion was scheduled to discuss the transcripts of the interviews in order to assure that the transcriptions were accurate portrayals of the lived experiences of the participants. Public reports of hospitals that have evaluated the impact of mentoring on professional advancement of minorities were also reviewed to explore the role of a formal mentoring program in a hospital.

The methodology that was used in this study is considered to be the most appropriate design because qualitative case studies "investigate a contemporary phenomenon within its real-life context" (Yin, 1994, p. 13). Additionally, a qualitative case study provides an in-depth investigation that results in details based on the participants' views (Yin, 1994). According to Yin, interviewing participants for a qualitative case study is a primary source of evidence. Therefore, a semicontrolled interview format was used to provide an opportunity for the interviewer to ask open-ended questions in order to gain insight about events that occurred in the participants' professional careers (Yin, 1994).

Significance of the Problem

The significance of this problem to leadership is apparent in organizations in which there is a lack of diversity as a result of insufficient support and resources for minority healthcare professionals. Racial minority groups have reported an inability to identify with their colleagues due to racial differences; therefore a sense of frustration and disconnect in working relationships becomes evident (Thomas, 2001). Racial diversity at the highest level of the organization is necessary in order for the organization to have patient care providers and members of the leadership team who are representative of the community that is being served (Pieper, 2004).

This problem is also significant to hospital organizations that provide services to a racially diverse patient population. This is important because as the number of African Americans living in the United States continues to increase, it is essential to have representation of this minority group at all levels of the organization (Larson, 2006). "Boards have to become more diverse first and foremost. Once you have a diverse board, individuals of color will be comfortable to apply for management positions" (Larson, 2006, p. 14).

It is uncertain if the current discomfort is due to the inability of African Americans to identify with their superiors and colleagues or if it is a result of the lack of opportunities to advance up the corporate ladder. The American College of Healthcare Executives (ACHE) and the NCHL both reported that mentoring may be an important factor in helping minorities advance to decision-making positions. However, there are limited data regarding the impact of mentoring on career advancement in healthcare specifically for African Americans ("A Race Ethnicity Comparison," 2002; *The Black Perspective Online, 2000)*.

It has been reported that there are continued efforts to increase diversity in healthcare, especially in hospitals. These efforts have been unsuccessful because there continues to be a lag in the number of minorities, specifically African American hospital chief executive officers (CEOs), chief nursing officers (CNOs), directors of nursing, and hospital executives. The number of African American CEOs nationwide has remained in the single digits (Hellinghausen, 2000; Sanders & Bowcutt, 2004). These results remain unchanged despite initiatives implemented by organizations such as ACHE to increase the number of minorities working in healthcare.

The research explored the importance of mentoring based on the lived experiences of African American healthcare professionals in becoming senior managers with the intention of advancing to an executive-level position. Stokes (2003) identified one function of a mentor as providing exposure and visibility for the protégé. Exploring the perception of mentoring and its influence on professional advancement also helped to determine if having a mentor in a decision-making position plays a significant role in motivating African Americans in their quest for career advancement.

As a result of the benefits that are seen with mentoring in other professions, the role of the mentor has become common in the corporate world in an effort to recruit and retain minorities, and it is believed that this may be applicable to healthcare (Ralston, 2003). According to a report in *The Black Perspective Online* (2000), "the coaching program builds on the belief that individual mentoring and coaching is an important part of the professional development for all healthcare managers, and is particularly essential to the career progression of minorities" (¶ 5). "In a diversity-driven mentoring program, protégés will prepare for their own career success and learn about the process, responsibilities, and qualifications necessary to be an effective leader" (Ambrose, 2003, ¶ 4).

Nature of the Study

This qualitative case study was designed to provide a better understanding of the career accomplishments of African American healthcare administrators and executives through exploration of their lived experiences as they relate to mentoring and perceived difficulties in advancing to executive positions within their career fields. A qualitative case study was conducted using a non-random selection to identify participants for the study. An initial group of study participants was asked to participate in the study.

These participants are professional colleagues of the study investigators. Other participants were identified using a snowball method of sampling. This process is conducted through a referral process. Initial participants were asked to refer other participants representative of the population that was being investigated.

Data were collected through tape recorded interviews using open-ended questions in a semi-structured format. This method of data collection is considered to be the best approach to collect accurate in-depth responses of the participants (Yin, 1994). The open-ended question semi-structured interview focused on the tenure of the employee, the perceived role and benefits of a mentor, and the employee's perception of the mentor's role in his or her professional advancement. In addition, perceived barriers to career advancement were addressed.

A qualitative case study design provided an opportunity to explore historical events that occurred in the careers of the participants. In this qualitative research, data were collected and common themes were identified. This method of data collection provided an opportunity to collect and interpret text data based on the recollection of the participants. A qualitative research design also provided an effective method of data collection.

This design was appropriate for this study because the semi-structured interview process of data collection provided an interactive environment in which the participants were asked general, open-ended questions. The responses to the questions were explored in detail to better understand the phenomenon that was being evaluated. In contrast to a quantitative research design, qualitative studies explore a phenomenon and avoid microanalysis of data based on a structured data collection process (Creswell, 2003). This research style was appropriate for this study because it allowed data collection from a purposeful sample of individuals who could provide detailed descriptions of their lived experiences, therefore ensuring that the results are representative of the population.

Data Collection

Data were obtained from interviews that focused on the lived experiences of 21 African American healthcare decision makers. The questions for the interview focused on mentoring and career advancement in the field of healthcare. The sample was a purposive sample in which various methods were used to identify members of this specific and difficult-to-reach population. This method of sampling permitted the selection of individuals who were specific to the population being evaluated and could therefore provide the most in-depth and informative responses to the interview questions.

African American hospital decision makers were identified using a referral process. This referral process is known as a snowball method of population sampling. This process involves identifying an initial group of participants who are representative of the population. This initial population then refers another subgroup representative of the population (Heckathorn, 2002).

The initial group of study participants was selected from a group of professional healthcare executives who were then employed in decision-making positions and were professional colleagues of the study investigator. The places of employment of the participants were not identified during the data collection process or in the results. Information that could identify the organization was not collected or included in the study results. All participants were asked to provide information specific to their lived experiences.

Requests for participation were made by e-mailing an introductory letter to potential participants to request participation in the study and to provide a brief overview of the study and the study population (see Appendix A). Participants were selected without regard to their experience of having or not having a mentor. Instead, each participant was selected based on the following criteria: African American, 18 years or older, employed in a decision-making position at a director's level or above within a hospital or inpatient care center, and willingness to participate in the study.

The interview questions for this study were not used previously in this population. Therefore, a pilot study was conducted with three participants who were representative of the study population. The pilot study provided face validity for the questions that were used during the interview. Based on the answers to the questions in the pilot study, appropriate changes were made in order to make the questions more understandable and to assure that their intent was appropriate (Moustakas, 1994). After completion of the interview, the data were compiled and analyzed to determine common themes and perceptions using a modified van Kaam method (Moustakas, 1994).

Analysis

After the open-ended questions, semistructured interview of each participant was completed, transcribed, and verified for accuracy. Then a follow up discussion was conducted, during which the transcription and general theme of the interview were presented to each participant. This second follow up allowed participants to comment on the responses captured during the interview in order to assure that the transcript of the interview was an accurate depiction of their lived experiences. In order to reduce bias in the analysis, the data analysis was conducted by a third party using a modified van Kaam method of analysis (Moustakas, 1994).

A modified van Kaam method of analysis analyzes qualitative data by clustering and identifying common themes in the responses of the study participants through the following process: (a) identify and validate the invariant constituents, (b) create a description of each participant's experience then develop a composite of each individual's experience, and (c) combine it with all the experiences to represent a general theme describing the experiences of all participants in the group (Moustakas, 1994).

Research Questions

In this research, the central phenomenon of mentoring among African American healthcare professionals was explored. The two central questions that this research explored were as follows:

1. What is the perceived role of mentoring in the professional advancement of African American healthcare professionals to decision-making positions? In order to understand whether mentoring plays a role in professional advancement, it was important to explore the perceptions of those professionals who have and those who have not been mentored during their careers.
2. What is the perception of healthcare professionals regarding the importance of mentorship and empowerment in their own professional advancement?

These questions provided subjective information from the participants regarding their views of mentoring and the importance, if any, that mentoring may have had in their careers.

Theoretical Framework

Organizational leaders in healthcare have a significant role and responsibility not only to the members of their organization but also to the members of the community they serve, and to the patients who receive their services. Leaders and leadership in the organization are directly related to the organization's culture and social infrastructure (Larson, 2006). As the organization grows and new leaders emerge, the culture of the organization must also change to develop leaders who are representative of the internal and external customers. Consequently, the evaluation and reward of individuals who are identified as effective leaders are determined by the organization's philosophy (Larson, 2006; Voges, 2006). Therefore, the philosophy of the organization affects the leadership and, more importantly, it has an effect on who the future leaders and decision makers will be.

The philosophy and vision of the organization is also important in helping to determine the organization's long-term vision and culture. In order to develop a leadership team in a healthcare organization that is representative of successful businesses in America, gender and ethnic diversity are a necessity in the organization's culture and strategic plan ("Strategies for Leadership," n.d.). For minorities seeking professional advancement in healthcare, the need for role modeling may be necessary for optimal performance in a work environment where there may be a lack of ethnic identity in upper management. Employees may need to be transformed into leaders in order to be professionally prepared for their next level of management.

Healthcare leaders require motivation and empowerment to be effectively transformed into a role that follows the five levels of Maslow's hierarchy of needs, in which self-actualization is the ability to "become everything a person is capable of being" (Longest, Rakich, & Darr, 2000, p. 775). For some individuals, this may be a desire to reach the highest level of management in the organization. Motivation for self-actualization and reaching the pinnacle of one's career requires guidance and support from someone who is highly respected and possesses strong leadership characteristics.

McClelland's learned needs theory can also be used to describe the needs of individuals who have a desire to become successful in their careers. McClelland's theory states that there are three basic needs that each highly motivated individual has and these needs must be met in order for individuals to reach self-actualization (Longest et al., 2000). The three needs are as follows: "The need for achievement, the need for power, the need for affiliation, including the need to associate with others, to form and sustain friendly and close interpersonal relationships, and to avoid conflicts" (Longest et al., p. 779). It is believed that these needs are not innate but instead are acquired over time according to the individual's environmental and situational exposure.

The need for close interpersonal relationships, specifically with other healthcare leaders, is essential for timely advancement up the corporate ladder (Gonzalez-Figueroa & Young, 2006; Larson, 2006). Self-actualization is necessary not only for minorities who are in the transformational process of becoming a leader but also for all motivated individuals who intend to achieve the highest attainable position within the organization (Longest et al., 2000). Maslow's hierarchy of needs, which includes self-actualization as the highest level of achievement, may be similar to career advancement. Promotion to the executive level position of an organization may be considered *self-actualization* of one's professional achievement. Figure 1 is a modification of Maslow's hierarchy of needs to represent the needs of minorities in healthcare.

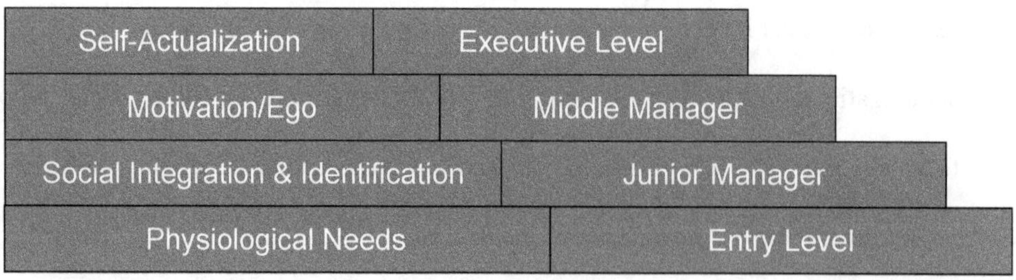

Figure 1. Hierarchical needs of minorities in healthcare adapted from Maslow (1943).

Leadership Theories

Many leadership theories are applicable to the advancement of motivated individuals working within a healthcare organization (Longest et al., 2000). The common trend in most of the leadership models is that "leadership is a process of one individual influencing another individual or group to achieve a particular objective" (Longest et al., 2000, p. 759). The Path-Goal Model of Leadership (Longest et al., 2000) incorporates various leadership behaviors such as situational, supportive, participative, and achievement-oriented leadership in order to provide coaching and professional guidance which lead to improved achievement among professionals. The application of these four leadership behaviors provides an opportunity to blend traits, skills, power, and behavior to meet the situation (Longest et al., 2000).

These leadership behaviors allow flexibility to mentors and coaches so they can provide the most effective method of mentoring regardless of the situation. This method of support is necessary, especially in a healthcare organization where there are many areas of diversity, particularly at the middle and lower levels of management. The implementation of such a model, or one that is similar to the Path-Goal Model, may be supportive in working with a diverse group of individuals who are being mentored by individuals required to make personality changes so that they can adapt to the mentees' methods of learning and leadership.

Early identification of subordinates with leadership abilities, or those with the motivation to succeed in the organization, is important. These individuals' characteristics and situational needs should be determined and the appropriate leadership behavior should be implemented in collaboration with mentoring. The mentor should be capable of developing the subordinate to his or her desired career level in the organization.

Careful implementations of these steps are important in assisting the subordinate to achieve his or her goals and level of performance (see Figure 1). Diversity awareness should be included as an important tool when mentoring individuals from other cultures and ethnicity. This allows both the mentor and mentee to have a favorable outcome, successful working relationship, and the adaptability and support necessary to achieve a common goal (Longest et al., 2000).

Definition of Terms

Words with unusual definitions or those that may have multiple meanings in the English language that are used throughout the study will be defined. The definition of all terms unique to this study, region, profession, or other qualifier will also be defined.

African American: The term African American was used to describe all members of the Black race. Black Hispanic, Black Caribbean, Black American and any individual who considers him or herself to be of Black descent are included in this definition.

Coaching: Providing technical advice while explaining how to complete a task (Thomas, 2001).

Decision-making position (decision maker): "Deciding on important matters: the process of making choices or reaching conclusions, especially on important political or business matters" (*Encarta Dictionary Tool*s, 2006). This title will includes any person who is employed in a management position in which that individual has decision-making responsibilities for the department. These responsibilities may include people management, candidate selection and termination, budgetary responsibilities, reports to an executive committee, or being a member of the executive committee. These individuals also make decisions that affect the culture and daily business operation of the organization.

Diversity: "The condition of being diverse; especially the inclusion of diverse people (as people of different races or cultures) in a group or organization" (Merriam-Webster Online, 2007).

Formal Mentoring: Provides detailed guidance to the mentor and protégée, outlining roles and responsibilities of each person participating in the mentoring process. "A formal mentoring program provides greater organizational control over the objectives, activities, and roles involved in a mentor-protégé relationship" (Tourigny & Pulich, 2005, p. 70). This type of mentoring process is representative of the culture and expectations of the organization. There is a high level of organizational involvement and, therefore, both the mentor and protégé benefit from the process through organizational recognitions. The duration of a formal mentoring process varies and may last from six months to a year (Tourigny & Pulich, 2005).

Heterogeneous Mentoring: Mentoring between individuals in which both mentor and protégé belong to different ethnic groups.

Homogeneous Mentor: Mentoring between individuals in which both mentor and protégé belong to the same ethnic group.

Human Resource Representative: A representative of the human resources department who works closely with the employees of the organization and has administrative responsibilities regarding personnel files.

Informal Mentoring: Less structured than formal mentoring and is formed by a mutual identification with developmental needs of someone within the organization. In an informal mentoring process, there are no contracts between the mentor and protégé. This relationship may last from one to several years, according to the individual's need. An informal mentoring process may take place between a manager or supervisor and a subordinate, or it may be a peer-to-peer relationship (Tourigny & Pulich, 2005).

Inpatient Care Facility: A healthcare organization that provides medical care to patients in an inpatient setting. This includes but is not limited to a nursing home or any chronic care setting.

Instructional Mentoring: Involves providing advice about completing a task that the protégé might not be comfortable performing. This method of mentoring does not provide the protégé with skills needed to advance to the executive level. During instructional mentoring, the protégé and the mentor do not develop the relationship to improve the protégé's confidence and competence. Therefore both individuals lack the closeness seen in other methods of mentoring (Thomas, 2001).

Leadership Team: Members of the highest level of the organization, including the vice president, chief financial officer, chief executive officer, chief nursing officer, or any member of the executive team.

Mentor: "Experienced adviser and supporter: somebody, usually older and more experienced, who advises and guides a younger, less experienced person" (*Encarta Dictionary Tools*, 2006). "Mentors can help young people overcome obstacles, nurture their strengths, and set them on the path of life with important skills" (Bernstein, 2007, p. 9).

Mentoring: Focuses on skills a mentor uses to develop a protégé to perform to his or her highest potential, leading to career advancement. The focus of mentoring is on the career of a protégé who is identified as a high performer and capable of advancement. This is in contrast to coaching that provides suggestions on improving performance and not career advancement (Fracaro, 2006, p. 13). "Mentoring refers to a set of roles performed by a mentor toward a protégé and activities that take place as part of the mentor-protégé relationship" (Tourigny & Pulich, 2005, p. 70). Kram (1985) stratified the key functions of mentoring into career functions and psychological functions. Career function includes "sponsorship, exposure and visibility, coaching, protection, and challenging assignment" (p. 29), whereas physiological function includes "role modeling, acceptance and confirmation, counseling and friendship" (Kram, 1985, p. 33).

Protégé (mentee): "One who is protected or trained or whose career is furthered by a person of experience, prominence, or influence" (Merriam-Webster Online, 2007).

Southeastern United States: Florida, Georgia, Tennessee, Texas, South Carolina, and Alabama.

Assumptions

The collection of data in a recorded session using a study interview format, whether in person or otherwise, may present some limitations with the responses obtained. It was assumed that the responses obtained during the interview were an accurate recollection based on the events that took place during the career of the individuals who were being interviewed. The following is a list of assumptions that were considered while collecting and evaluating the data.

1. All participants provided truthful responses.

2. The role of the mentor in the participants' career is accurate according to the definition of a mentor as outlined above.
3. The research participants' responses were accurately interpreted.
4. The perceptions of the participants are an accurate representation of their true lived experiences.
5. Questions in the open-ended interview were not biased and led toward a certain response set.
6. Questions asked were clear and easily understood by the participants.

Each participant was given the opportunity to participate in the interview in a place that provided comfort and privacy. The participants were also assured that the information they provided will remain confidential. Additionally, there were no unique identifiers that would reveal the participants' identities. To ensure accurate interpretation of the responses, a follow up was conducted after the interviews were transcribed. The purpose of the follow up discussion was to allow participants to comment on the transcription of their interview in order to assure that the transcriptions were an accurate depiction of their lived experiences.

Limitations

There were several potential limitations in evaluating the professional impact of mentoring for African American healthcare professionals employed in decision-making positions. An apparent limitation was the lack of available data to quantify the number of African American healthcare executives nationwide. It has been reported that African Americans comprise 5% of the total number of healthcare executives, with only 1% employed at the CEO level (Gathers, 2003; Griffin, 2001; Hellinghausen, 2000; Woog,

2005). Information regarding the total number of African American healthcare executives employed in a hospital setting was unavailable. The total number of African American healthcare executives was determined based on the total number of chief executives employed in medical and surgical hospitals with 1% of this population extrapolated to represent African Americans (Griffin, 2001; U.S. Department of Labor, 2006).

Access to the study participants was also a limitation in this study. For this reason, the data were collected from a geographical region that has large metropolitan cities with a high prevalence of African American residents. It was believed to be more likely for metropolitan cities with large healthcare organizations to have African American hospital decision makers employed in positions at the director level or higher. Therefore, the sample group was selected from individuals living in the southeastern United States. The number of responses and method of data collection was also expected to be a limitation and could be viewed as potentially biased based on the nonrandom sampling and sample size.

Each participant was expected to provide a truthful response to each question. Due to the various interpretations of mentoring, especially in a hospital setting, it was possible that each individual might have had a different definition of a mentor. Each participant might have interpreted the mentoring process and the impact on his or her professional advancement differently. Prior to the commencement of each interview, the definition of a mentor was provided. The purpose of providing a definition was to assist the participants in providing accurate responses. Other perceived limitations of the study were as follows:

1. The honesty of each participant response during the interview.

2. The amount of time available to collect and analyze the data.
3. The validity of the interview questions used.
4. The number of African Americans working in healthcare in a decision-making capacity in the southeastern United States; data may not be generalizable to a different population.
5. This group of participants may not be a true representation of the population; therefore the results may only be representative of African American healthcare professionals in the southeastern United States.

Delimitations

This study was confined to interviewing African Americans in decision-making positions. Included were all individuals in middle management, from a director-level position to those at the highest level of the organization, in which the outline of their responsibilities includes at least one of the following: employing and terminating employees, managing a departmental budget, creating and presenting an executive report for the leadership team, and making executive decisions regarding the operation of a department. Individuals were identified based on their participation in leadership and professional organizations, professional references, and through the human resources department in each hospital.

Data for the study were collected by interviewing 21 individuals who were employed in a hospital or inpatient care facility. These individuals were employed in decision-making roles and were responsible for making business or medical decisions that directly affected the organization's goals and objectives. This study focused on the mentoring of African Americans and the impact of mentoring on career advancement for African Americans hospital executives.

Summary

Chapter 1 outlined the problem statement, purpose and nature of the study, definition of operational terms, assumptions, limitations, and theoretical framework of the study. This introductory chapter provided insight that diversity in healthcare is important in order for the organization to achieve its goals and objectives. However, effective leadership also includes careful selection of individuals who can represent the organization's internal and external customers. The workplace, including healthcare organizations such as hospitals and other patient care organizations, provides services to a group of ethnically diverse individuals. It is the responsibility of the leaders of the organization to provide and implement leadership behaviors that members of all levels of the organization can use to support their professional development.

The following chapter provides a review of the literature outlining diversity in healthcare, the role of mentoring in career advancement, and the prevalence of African Americans in decision-making positions. Chapter 2 also expands on the concept that diversity is important in organizational leadership, and mentoring may be beneficial to minorities who aspire to advance to an executive level within the organization. Therefore, all employees who have the desire to advance professionally in the organization should have access to mentors or role models who can assist them in achieving this goal. African Americans are often faced with the challenge of not having the resources to assist them with their desires for professional advancement (McGlowan-Fellows & Thomas, 2005;

Thomas, 2001). Careful implementation of mentoring relationships may be an effective method of meeting the developmental needs of this group.

CHAPTER 2: REVIEW OF THE LITERATURE

A better understanding of the literature regarding the empowerment of African Americans to decision-making positions in healthcare is necessary in order to determine the role of mentoring in professional advancement. Chapter 1 provided the background to the problem. Chapter 2 provides an historical perspective of the role of mentoring in career advancement, current findings about mentoring and minorities, career opportunities for African American healthcare workers, and the need for diversity in healthcare.

Documentation

An extensive review of the literature regarding the number of African Americans employed in an executive-level position in the healthcare industry was completed and it was determined that the data on this topic are limited. A search was conducted using the University of Phoenix library database, EBSCOhost and ProQuest, and the World Wide Web search engine using the following search terms: African American executives, African American and mentoring, mentoring in healthcare, mentoring, minorities, mentoring minorities, mentoring and Blacks, healthcare workers, mentoring professional advancement, minority healthcare workers, and healthcare executives. The review of the available data revealed that not only was there limited information on African American executives in healthcare, but the number of African Americans working in the healthcare industry who were promoted to a management level seldom advanced to an executive level ("A Race Ethnicity Comparison," 2002; Gathers, 2003; Thomas, 2001).

Literature Review

Midlevel managers and executives are the most influential employees in the hospital and are key contributors to the growth of the organization (Pappas, Flaherty, & Wooldridge, 2003). Most decisions pertaining to the success of the organization are conducted at a director level or above. In healthcare settings, particularly hospitals, most entry-level managers do not have the autonomy to make decisions that will have an impact on the success of the organization (Gwyther, 2006). The available data that pertain to the mentoring of African Americans employed in healthcare are specific to healthcare disciplines such as nursing and general healthcare. However, there are no specific data that stratify healthcare workers into the various healthcare disciplines such as medicine, pharmacy, or health administration. Therefore, it is difficult to quantify the impact of mentoring on these specific areas.

References have been made to mentoring in healthcare as well as other industries, and there appears to be a professional benefit to mentoring employees at all levels of the organization (Thomas, 2001). Other reports have outlined the benefits of diversity in healthcare, but the benefit of mentoring African Americans from the beginning of employment to the advancement to a decision-making position is poorly documented (Gonzalez-Figueroa & Young, 2005; Larson, 2006; Worth, 2004). The questions that were intended to be answered in this research are as follows:

1. What is the perceived role of mentoring in the professional advancement of African American healthcare professionals to decision-making positions?
2. What is the perception of healthcare professionals regarding the importance of mentorship and empowerment in their own professional advancement?

The potential benefit of this research was to provide increased awareness concerning the role of a mentor in empowering African Americans working in the hospital and inpatient sector of the healthcare industry. Additionally, another important benefit was to identify obstacles encountered by African Americans as they advance in their careers as healthcare professionals. In response to the need for accurate documentation of African Americans in healthcare, the African American Nurses Association (AANA) has recently implemented initiatives that will provide more accurate documentation of minority healthcare nurses (Worth, 2004).

Documentation and validation of diversity is necessary because as the U.S. population increases, communities have become more diverse ("Strategies for Leadership," n.d.). Consequently, in order for hospitals to remain competitive changes are needed in employee selection to include and increase diversity in the healthcare team. The American College of Healthcare Executives (ACHE) has identified the lack of diversity and has made recommendations to increase diversity in healthcare ("A Race Ethnicity Comparison," 2002). Minority healthcare executives reported that mentoring in healthcare is necessary in order to create a more diverse executive team (Voges, 2006).

The literature confirms that there is a disparity in the number of African Americans in healthcare leadership. Additionally, a higher percentage of men advance to decision-making positions as compared to females (Gathers, 2003). Although the rate of promotion is not the same for African American males as it is for Caucasians males, African American males continue to be promoted more rapidly when compared to African American females.

Historical Perspective

Career Opportunities for African Americans in Healthcare

Diversity has become a major focus for organizational leaders. Thus, there have been reports on the need to have adequate representation of minority employees at all levels of the organization to reflect diversity in the organization's culture (Gathers, 2003; Neil, 2003; "Strategies for Leadership," n.d.). Members of the healthcare industry have also recognized that there has been a change in the ethnic demographics of the customers who are being served, and there is a growing need for those customers to be able to identify with members of the organization where services are rendered ("Strategies for Leadership," n.d.).

In the early 1960s, approximately 60% of U.S. employees were Caucasian males. However, at the end of 2005, Caucasian males represented 40% of the workforce, which suggests an increase in the number of minorities in the workforce (Gathers, 2003). The increase in minority workers provided increased advancement opportunities for minorities.

Yet while there are more minorities in management-level positions, there continue to be few minorities promoted to senior-level and executive-level positions. The disparity of minorities in senior level positions is also evident in the healthcare industry, and even though other industries are experiencing rapid improvement in diversity, the healthcare industry continues to make slow progress in the promotion of minorities beyond entry level-management positions. This is evident by the low percentage employed at the top levels of healthcare; today the number of minority healthcare executives remains in the single digits (Gathers, 2003).

A recent study conducted by ACHE, in collaboration with several healthcare organizations, reported that African Americans face challenges in achieving upper level positions as compared to Caucasians (Weil, 2003). Additionally, African American women are compensated at an annual rate of 14% less than Caucasian women. This reflects an overall reduction of 3% in the average salary for African Americans since 1997 (Weil, 2003).

In spite of several reports on the slow advancement of minorities, overall there has been some level of success in improving diversity in various areas in the workplace. However, much work is needed in order to have fair representation, equal opportunity for career advancement, and compensation for African Americans (Lockwood, 2005; Thomas, 2001; Weil, 2003). Based on the available literature, it is uncertain why there is a slow improvement in racial diversity in the healthcare industry. Despite this slow progress, most workers agree that diversity is important for the success of the organization (Lockwood, 2005; Weil, 2003).

Diversity in Healthcare

It is estimated that by the year 2050 minorities will make up 90% of the total population (Neil, 2003). Large minority groups such as African Americans, Hispanics/Latinos, and American Indians represent one fourth of the total population in the U.S. healthcare industry. Because of the increased diversity in the general population, hospitals continue to provide services to a diverse group of individuals (Neil, 2003).

There continues to be consistent underrepresentation of these groups in healthcare management (Woog, 2005). Increasing racial diversity among healthcare workers and the healthcare management team is necessary to prepare leaders of the healthcare industry to adequately respond to the diversity needs of their customers. A lack of diversity among healthcare individuals in hospitals that serve a large diverse population can result in financial loss to the organization (Evans, 2004).

Hospital administrators must understand the potential financial implications if there is a delayed or absent response to the needs of their customers. Having a diverse group across all levels of the organization is the key to the organization's success (Evans, 2004; Voges, 2006). Today, one of the greatest demands of healthcare consumers is the ability to identify with individuals who are providing their care. Recommendations have been made by key decision-making leaders in the healthcare workforce to develop strategies that will improve diversity in healthcare (Evans, 2004; Scott, 2006).

It is important to identify the need for diversity at all levels of employment, including the highest level of management. The lack of promotion of African Americans to upper level management positions is evidenced by the small percentage (2%-5%) of minorities who are represented at the senior level (Woog, 2005). During the previous decade, minorities represented approximately 28% of all healthcare workers. In spite of this, the number of minorities advancing to decision-making positions has consistently trailed behind the number of Caucasians who have advanced to senior management positions (Evans, 2004; Woog, 2005). The number of African American women in senior level positions is poorly represented in comparison to Caucasian women (Gathers, 2003).

A recent report by Evans (2004) stated that the minority population of registered nurses in the United States is predominantly American Indians, Hispanics, and African Americans. These groups represent a small percentage of professionals and decision makers in this profession. According to a recent survey of the top 22 nursing schools nationwide, only 7.3% of the 15,340 nursing students were African American (Anonymous, 2004/2005).

The overall numbers of minorities in other healthcare groups are also in single digits (Evans, 2004; Late, 2004). Similar to the low number of minority nurses, 6.8% and 6.1- 6.7% of the nation's dentists and physicians, respectively, belong to a minority group (Evans, 2004; Gartland, Hojat, Christian, Callahan, & Nasca, 2003). Although there are a large number of African Americans who are currently employed in healthcare, the overall number of minorities in the industry consistently lags behind the number of Caucasians who are entering the workforce. Not only is there slow advancement of African Americans to upper level positions, but this trend is also seen in the recruitment of African Americans in healthcare (Anonymous, 2004/2005).

Prevalence of Minorities in Healthcare

Currently one in every four Americans belongs to a minority group, and minority groups are expected to continue growing during the next several years ("A Race Ethnicity Comparison," 2002). Despite the awareness for an increase in diversity in the healthcare industry, only 2-5% of healthcare executives are African American, and only 1% of those executives are at a CEO level (Griffin, 2001; Woog, 2005). In 1997, 32% of African American women were employed in managerial positions compared to 44% of Hispanics (Gathers, 2003).

The number of African Americans employed as general managers is partially due to the higher percentage of African American males working in healthcare management (Gathers, 2003). In 1997, African American males represented 42% of workers in general management positions compared to 56% Caucasian males. While these percentages appear to be promising, reports from national studies have indicated that few African Americans are employed in top management positions (Gathers, 2003; Woog, 2005).

African Americans are often compensated significantly lower for the same job as compared to their Caucasian colleagues (Gathers, 2003). To successfully increase racial diversity at the executive level in the hospital setting, a detailed strategy is needed that includes improving diversity during the hiring process, mentoring minorities to advance beyond entry-level positions, and increasing diversity awareness in the hospital industry (Institute for Diversity in Health Management, 2006). The AANA has identified the need for accurate documentation of the number of African Americans, specifically nurses, employed in healthcare.

According to the Bureau of Labor and Statistics, there are 85,290 medical and health services managers employed in a medical or surgical hospital. Of these, 5,890 are chief executives (U.S. Department of Labor, 2006). This report does not specify the number of African Americans employed as chief executives.

Diversity awareness and improvement in minority representation nationwide is important; adequate representation is often seen in underserved communities where there is routinely an overrepresentation of African Americans and other minorities employed in healthcare. The mentoring and promotion of African Americans and other minorities at all levels of healthcare is one of the key initiatives outlined by ACHE, American Hospital Association (AHA), and National Center for Healthcare Leadership (NCHL) (Institute for Diversity and Health Management, 2006). Subsequently, the Institute for Diversity and Health Management has outlined strategies to improve the number of minorities in healthcare and to support their advancement to senior management positions within the healthcare industry (Institute for Diversity and Health Management, 2006; Worth, 2004).

Healthcare Organizations

Importance of Diversity in Healthcare

Diversity has become a focus as the American population increases and members of different cultures become more integrated into society (Neil, 2003). As the evolution of diversity unfolds, hospital administrators have recognized the importance of diversity in order to remain the market leader. In 2002, spending in the healthcare industry exceeded $1.6 trillion. This growth is the fastest in the U.S. economy (Szabo, 2004). Communities are growing and becoming more diverse, thus members of the healthcare team must become representatives for the communities that they serve.

A diverse workplace is necessary because, regardless of the location of the hospital, patients are more comfortable when they are being serviced in an institution where diversity is evident throughout the organization (Neil, 2003). The importance of identifying the needs for diversity and adequate representation of African Americans at all levels of management will provide an insight into which strategies are needed to create an environment where African Americans can advance to the highest levels of the hospital organization. These strategies will provide support to the hospital in recruiting and retaining not only minority employees but also gaining the patronage of minorities seeking healthcare services.

Increasing racial diversity in the workplace will provide a sense of community partnership for members of the organization. The hospital sector of the healthcare industry has the potential to become the leader in diversity awareness by providing opportunities for African Americans and other minorities (Neil, 2003). The leadership team in the hospital should be comprised of a diverse group of individuals to represent members of various ethnic groups. Otherwise, hospital executives who fail to identify and embrace the need for diversity may experience difficulty gaining the support from members of the communities they serve (Neil, 2003).

Key Decision Makers

Healthcare providers from many specialties compose the leadership team in a hospital setting. However, the key members of the healthcare leadership team in the hospitals included in this study were leaders in the following specialties: pharmacy, medicine, nursing, and administration. Each decision maker employed in these specialty areas plays an important role in the daily operation of the organization.

The pharmacy director and vice president of pharmacy services are key decision makers at the executive level and participate in the leadership decision making process. The director of pharmacy has complex responsibilities that include making major decisions pertaining to the hospital's pharmacy formulary, management of the pharmacy's budget, and working cohesively with a multidisciplinary team (Nold & Sander, 2004). Additionally, the director of pharmacy and the vice president of pharmacy services must possess skills that will help the organization to provide high quality care to patients, thereby assisting the hospital to achieve its goals and objectives (Ivey, 2005).

The nursing director and vice president of nursing services are also important decision makers in the hospital because the nursing division represents more than 50% of a hospital's total operating cost. Other leadership positions held by nurses in hospitals are director of nursing finance and manager of nursing operations (Zachary, Gilbert, &

Gragg, 1995). African Americans and other minorities seldom hold these decision-making positions. Minorities working in these leadership positions are poorly represented, which may be due to the overall low prevalence of minority groups in healthcare executive positions (Griffin, 2001).

The medical director's role in the hospital is equally as important as that of the pharmacy director and nursing director. The medical director's decisions directly affect the level of patient care provided and medical services that will be available to patients. This directly impacts the reputation of the organization and its potential for growth. The nursing, pharmacy, and medical decision makers in the hospital are essential to the daily operation and long-term success of the organization.

Prevalence of African Americans in Medicine, Pharmacy, and Nursing

There are 233,000 licensed pharmacists in the United States and 22% are employed in a hospital setting. Surprisingly, African Americans make up only 3.1% of the number of pharmacists nationwide (*Bureau of Labor Statistics*, 2004; *Bureau of Labor Statistics*, n.d.). A more thorough investigation is needed to determine the causes for the low prevalence of African American pharmacists.

Currently there are approximately 2,464,000 registered nurses nationwide with 10.1% of this group represented by African Americans (*Bureau of Labor Statistics*, 2004). Similar to the pharmacy director and vice president of pharmacy services, the director of nursing/vice president of nursing services is one of the highest levels of nursing representation in the hospital and is responsible for developing sound financial strategies for the hospital (Nold & Sander, 2004). Nationwide, only 6.1% of licensed physicians are African Americans (*Bureau of Labor Statistics*, 2004). This small number does not provide many opportunities for mentoring young African Americans in the profession of medicine and, consequently, the low percentage of African Americans in the profession does not provide adequate role models for mentoring other African Americans into leadership roles.

The director of pharmacy, director of nursing, and the medical director are key decision makers in a hospital setting. A cohesive and collaborative working relationship among this group of individuals is instrumental in helping the organization to remain competitive, and for the healthcare providers to give the best quality care possible. The senior nursing executives are responsible for predicting the productivity of the hospital and providing cost analyses for the executive team (Zachary et al., 1995). The nursing director's responsibilities coupled with the pharmacy director's instructions regarding the cost of medication, medication distribution, and the management of the pharmacy budget provides expert guidance for the financial decisions made by the executive team (Ivey, 2005).

Recruitment of Healthcare Employees

Diversity in Recruitment Strategies

There are reports addressing the leadership of minorities in the healthcare industry ("A Race Ethnicity Comparison," 2002; Griffin, 2001). During the past 15 years, there have been major efforts to recruit nurses, physicians, and other healthcare providers from within the United States and foreign countries (Brush, Sochaiski, & Berger, 2004). Approximately 25% of the doctors and 14% of the nurses practicing in the United States are foreign born (Brush, et. al., 2004: "Fewer Foreign Docs," 2004). Because of this aggressive recruitment, there has been an increase in the representation of healthcare providers from various minority groups.

Gathers (2003) reported that minorities are well represented in the healthcare industry, but there is a lack of representation of minority groups at the executive level. Hellinghausen (2000) described a healthcare program called Health People 2010 that has implemented strategies to improve the number of minorities. This report provides a contradictory report to Gathers' findings and reports a misrepresentation of minorities in healthcare. The program initiatives by Health People 2010 will increase the number of African American nurses from 6.9% to 13% in 2010.

Many factors have contributed to the inadequate representation and professional advancement of minorities. One contributing factor to the inadequate representation and professional advancement of this group is that performance evaluations do not reflect the work ethics of African American employees. African Americans are required to be more qualified than their Caucasian counterparts for executive positions, and routinely Caucasians do not share development and career-related information with their African American counterparts (Gathers, 2003; Shur Bilchik, 2000). Based on the Gathers' report, it appears that African Americans do not have access to the same career opportunities as their Caucasian colleagues. Therefore, the purpose of this qualitative study was to determine if mentoring will provide a positive outcome for career advancement among African Americans.

Mentoring

Based on the literature, several styles and definitions of mentoring have been outlined; some approaches of mentoring are formal while others are informal (Tourigny

& Pulich, 2005). The mentoring process used in healthcare will be evaluated in order to determine if this leadership pathway helps to develop minorities into becoming future leaders. Mentoring and coaching are important to one's career success and according to *The Black Perspective Online* (2000), "the coaching program builds on the belief that individual mentoring and coaching is an important part of the professional development for all healthcare managers, and is particularly essential to the career progression of minorities" (¶ 5). "In a diversity-driven mentoring program, protégés will prepare for their own career success and learn about the process, responsibilities, and qualifications necessary to be an effective leader" (Ambrose, 2003, para.1).

Mentoring for minorities is being implemented in large nonhospital healthcare organizations such as Johnson & Johnson, ("Leadership Development Program", n.d.; "Supporting our diverse culture," n.d.) and Eli Lilly ("Affinity Groups," 2004) and may be the strategy needed to improve the advancement of minority healthcare providers to the executive-level of their organizations. Mentoring is important to career development especially in large organizations. Situations in which junior employees receive support or coaching from a senior employee often lead to early advancement in their careers (Gonzalez-Figueroa & Young, 2005).

Professional guidance through mentoring can result in a more positive outcome for the career of minorities than their Caucasian colleagues. However, minorities do not have equal access to or support from mentors as compared to other ethnic groups who are given mentoring opportunities. Minorities are routinely coupled with mentors who are not leaders in the organization, or may not be in a position to provide them with exposure to the key decision makers who are capable of influencing their careers (Gonzalez-Figueroa

& Young, 2005). The inability to identify with senior Caucasian members of the organization may also be one of the reasons why minorities may not have equal access to mentors (Gonzalez-Figueroa & Young, 2005). In situations where there is cross-race mentoring, both the mentor and the mentee may experience some social discomfort as a result of cultural differences (Gonzalez-Figueroa & Young, 2005).

Strategies to Improve the Advancement of Minorities in Healthcare

The disparities in representation of executive-level workers extend beyond ethnic boundaries. The lack of representation becomes more evident among minority females (Jandeska & Kraimer, 2005); there are significantly fewer females in CEO and upper level positions than males (Jandeska & Kraimer, 2005). The National Association of Health Services Executives (NAHSE) and ACHE have made several recommendations to improve the number of African Americans females in decision making positions. Among these recommendations are opportunities for executives to provide mentoring for minorities, to improve the awareness of career advancement opportunities in the institution, provide networking opportunities, and make available specific criteria for advancement to upper level positions ("A Race Ethnicity Comparison," 2002).

These recommendations are intended to improve minority representation in healthcare. One of the key factors to advancement is visibility and strategic self-marketing. Unfortunately, African American healthcare workers are unable to convince decision makers that they are the ideal candidates for senior management positions. Therefore, they are unable to advance up the corporate ladder as quickly as Caucasians with similar job experience or educational preparation ("A Race Ethnicity Comparison," 2002).

The requirement of a sponsor or mentor may be necessary to provide the added exposure that is needed to place African American employees who have the skills and experience to assume new and challenging positions. A sponsor or mentor will help these individuals to identify their strengths and provide opportunities in which they can market themselves to the appropriate person responsible for making career advancements decisions.

Career Plans for African Americans

A large number of African Americans have a definite career plan in place and most are expected to continue their career in a hospital setting ("A Race Ethnicity Comparison," 2002). It is not known how the decision to continue their careers in the hospital will change the current pattern that is evident in the hospital setting. The number of African Americans working in healthcare may not influence the number of African Americans who will advance to an executive-level position.

The projection, according to a recent report, revealed that the number of African Americans who aspire to become CEOs is lower than Caucasians and Hispanics ("A Race Ethnicity Comparison," 2002). African Americans represent the lowest percentage of all ethnic groups, except Asians, who aspire to be CEOs in hospitals. Many factors may contribute to the decision of African Americans to advance to executive positions.

The racial interaction between Caucasian supervisors and African American subordinates plays an important role. Minority managers are less likely to receive adequate support from the employees they supervise, and oftentimes their annual evaluations are not reflective of their daily job performance. In addition, Caucasian managers do not share important career-related information with minority managers ("A Race Ethnicity Comparison," 2002).

It is evident that there are concerns regarding the professional relationship between African American managers and their Caucasian supervisors. There is also a lack of support to assist with professional development, a lack of detailed outline of career opportunities, and the strategies for achieving them are not clearly stated. There is also a perception among minority groups (Hispanics, Asians, and African Americans) that Caucasian managers have better opportunities for career advancement than any other ethnic group ("A Race Ethnicity Comparison," 2002). This perception could have an impact on students at the collegiate level who are considering the possibility of choosing a career in healthcare. The slow growth in career advancement and small percentage of minorities in executive-level positions may be a potential deterrent for college students entering the healthcare industry (Evans, 2004).

There is a need for African American healthcare executives, and providing mentoring for African American managers may help to satisfy this need. Moreover, heterogeneous mentoring may be equally important in order to improve the working relationship between African Americans and Caucasians ("A Race Ethnicity Comparison," 2002). A better understanding of the work ethics and value that both ethnic groups can provide to the workplace will help to change the perception of African Americans in leadership positions, which will create new opportunities as well as promote diversity in hospitals nationwide.

Mentoring for Success

Overview of Mentoring

Mentoring is a common term used in the healthcare industry and is often used interchangeably with coaching. The lack of clarity in the definition of mentoring prevents a generalized acceptance of this process in healthcare. In the review of literature, there has not been a clear and concise definition of mentoring. For the purpose of this study, a mentor is considered to be

> someone who serves as an advisor or practical teacher with whom you intimately communicate about issues of a professional nature. And if you're fortunate, this may be a person you're already associated with, such as an instructor/practitioner you currently know or had a good connection with in the past. She or he possesses greater insight and more extensive experience in areas you want to strengthen (McCluskey, 2005, p. 3).

An informal approach of mentoring is usually conducted with an experienced individual providing expert advice to a junior healthcare worker; however, a more formal approach is needed in order to have generalized acceptance in healthcare (Dancer, 2003). Mentoring has been used in various settings to help individuals transition into new professional roles. During this process, the mentor provides information, advice, and support, and in turn builds a committed relationship with the mentee (North, Johnson, Knotts, & Whelan, 2006).

The purpose of the mentoring process is to provide a stimulating environment in order for the mentee to build a successful career. The primary benefit of the mentoring program is to assist the mentee to maximize his or her skills in order to become a high performer. Mentoring healthcare professionals not only improves performance but also helps to improve the development of highly skilled employees (Dancer, 2003). A successful mentoring process results in the mentee identifying strengths and areas of improvement and develops key strategies to make the necessary improvements. Effective mentoring is the key to the success of the healthcare organizations conducting business in the twenty-first century (Bohne, 2003; May, 2003).

During the mentoring process, it is the mentee who ultimately makes the decisions rather than the mentor. This is important because the mentee must agree with the plan of action as this final outcome will determine his or her professional or personal achievements. As the relationship between the mentor and the mentee matures, the role of the mentor may change in order to adjust to changes in situations. The mentor's role may change from coach to facilitator, or even a networker or role model. As changes occur in the mentor/mentee relationship, the mentee must adjust to these changes and be willing to commit to any new challenges (Dancer, 2003). Figure 2 outlines the life cycle of a mentoring relationship.

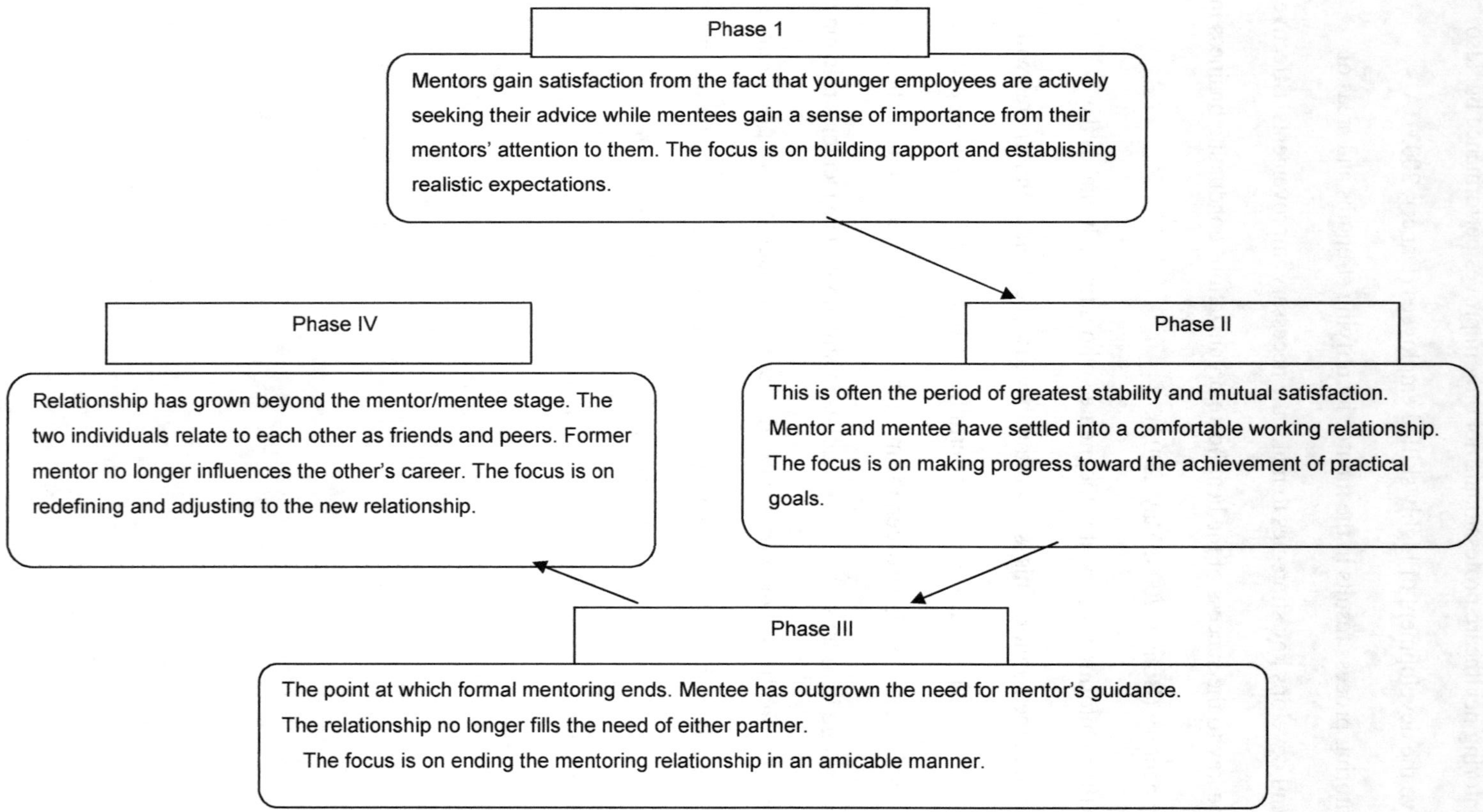

Figure 2. Life cycle of a mentoring relationship adapted from *Life Cycle of a Mentoring Relationship* by J. Kirk, 1991.

Mentoring in the Workplace

There is an increase in awareness that diversity is important in order to have a qualified group of employees who will provide the best services needed in the workplace (Rajan & Harris, 2003). The U.S. workforce will experience a new identity among the members of the executive team during the next 10 to 20 years as minorities outnumber the Caucasian employees (Voges, 2006). As these changes occur, the leadership team must determine how to prepare first-level managers to advance professionally in their careers in order to meet these new demands. Specific attention must be given to African Americans working in healthcare because this particular group often encounters roadblocks that prevent them from upper level advancement (Voges, 2006).

African Americans must also be recognized as high-level performers in order to be considered for advancement to an executive level in the healthcare organization. In order for African Americans to have professional guidance and the necessary exposure in the workplace, there should be a mentoring process in place (Larson, 2006; Voges, 2006). A formal mentoring program will improve the deficit of professional guidance that is currently available for African Americans. Professional guidance helps to improve the number of opportunities available for career advancement of African American healthcare providers employed in a hospital setting.

As the healthcare industry responds to the increased need for diversity, it is important that a multicultural workforce is implemented. In order to have a productive workforce that shares the organization's vision, there must be clear communication and understanding among all members of the leadership team (Washington, Erickson, & Ditomassi, 2004). Organizations such as Johnson & Johnson, a multibillion dollar healthcare organization, have initiated formal affinity groups to improve diversity within the organization. Johnson & Johnson, in response to the need for diversity in the workplace, has implemented several programs such as a leadership development program for graduates that provides mentoring and interaction with members of the senior management team ("Supporting our Diverse Culture" n.d.).

In addition to providing mentoring for individuals entering the workforce, Johnson & Johnson also has several formal diversity committees such as the African American Leadership Council (AALC). This group provides support, networking, and mentoring for individuals with common interests ("Supporting Diverse Cultures," n.d.). The leadership team of this international healthcare organization has also recognized that mentoring may be a key component for career advancement, especially for individuals of minority groups.

As organizational leaders work toward improving diversity and providing an environment in which their customers feel culturally comfortable, there must also be a representation of diversity at the executive level of management. This provides support and directions on cultural sensitivity. Mentoring a protégé for success can "directly impact protégé career advancement" (Tourigny & Pulich, 2005, p. 70). The support that it provides to the protégé gives guidance in regard to career planning in a direction that is in alignment with the organization's goals and objectives, but most importantly it provides exposure of the protégé to the appropriate individuals at the executive level (Tourigny & Pulich, 2005). The AALC's mission is to assist the organization (Johnson & Johnson) in having adequate representation of African Americans at every level of the organization and to provide professional support as they advance within the organization ("Leadership Development Program," n.d.; "Supporting Diverse Cultures," n.d.).

History of Mentoring

Throughout history there have been mentors who have assumed various roles such as teacher, counselor, master, protector, or advisor to young, inexperienced individuals. Mentoring can be traced back to the earlier years of Socrates, who served as a teacher to Plato and Aristotle, who taught Alexander the Great. Dr. Benjamin Mays mentored Dr. Martin Luther King, Jr.

In earlier years, a mentor was considered to be someone who was faithful and could be trusted to guide an inexperienced person on a journey to personal, professional, or career advancement (Bernstein, 2007). Early mentoring theories were based on the needs of Caucasian males because of the homogeneous group that was represented in leadership roles. The mentoring process at that time did not include diversity and therefore was not considered to be a good representation for other ethnic groups (Ragin, 1997).

Mentoring became popular during the 1970s, but many healthcare organizations did not readily implement programs in their organizations despite reports of the benefits of mentoring in the workplace. Diversity increased in corporate America as a result of the increased concentration of coaching from experts, while European businesses focused on personal development and learning as key to the mentoring process (Dancer, 2003). Today, many organizations have identified the benefits of a mentoring program and have included mentoring as a part of the developmental process for experienced as well as inexperienced workers (Dolan, 2004).

Advancement

Opportunity for African Americans Versus Caucasians

The racial imbalances that are seen at the executive level of many organizations are partially due to the inability to recruit and retain highly qualified minority employees. A common reason for poor retention is the lack of opportunity for advancement within the organization (Shur Bilchik, 2000; Thomas, 2001). In situations where African Americans have the opportunity to become members of the organization, there are similar patterns of career advancement for both African Americans and Caucasians in the corporate workforce.

Caucasians are usually identified as outstanding achievers early in their careers and are therefore placed on a fast track. In contrast, minority workers encounter many barriers. Qualified minority candidates face difficulties in securing job interviews even though they have the proper credentials and graduate degrees as well as experience and professional certifications (Shur Bilchik, 2000). Those who are fortunate enough to secure a position within the organization are often promoted to middle management and remain there for several years (Shur Bilchik, 2000).

The slow advancement to an executive-level position is often unrelated to their educational preparation, work experience, or job performance (Shur Bilchik, 2000; Thomas, 2001). For African Americans who are promoted to executive-level positions, those positions are usually related to some form of racially based duties such as community relations or other minority-related responsibilities (Thomas, 2001). Other minorities who are promoted to executive-level positions routinely wait several years longer than their Caucasian counterparts before they experience acceleration in their careers (Thomas, 2001). Some problems that have been identified as obstacles for African Americans being promoted or seeking employment in the healthcare industry are due to inexperience with diversity by the organization. These organizations may not be aware of the resources available to provide them with access to qualified African Americans; other organizational leaders do not enforce diversity among their employees even though there may be a diversity taskforce in place (Shur Bilchik, 2000).

Mentoring Minorities

Minorities experience many challenges related to the organization's enforcement of diversity. These challenges can have a negative effect on their professional advancement. Mentoring may play a role in reducing these challenges. However, there are also challenges that are related to the type of mentoring that minority healthcare workers receive that directly impact their professional advancement.

Minority professionals who progress at a slow rate to the executive level routinely receive instructional mentoring. Instructional mentoring, though beneficial, does not provide the necessary relationship and expertise that are required to become an executive. Instead, this type of mentoring only helps the mentee to develop better skills. In order for minorities to develop the confidence and gain the credibility that are needed to advance, it is important that their mentors not only provide coaching but also share technical advice and experiences and offer emotional support.

Mentoring for African Americans should be viewed as a developmental process in which individuals are being groomed and mentored for the next level of their careers. African Americans can also benefit from a diverse network of relationships. The network must be secure so that if the mentor is no longer a part of the network, the relationship with other members of the network does not suffer. Additionally, it is beneficial for minorities to have cross-race as well as cross-gender mentoring (Gonzalez-Figueroa & Young, 2005; Thomas, 2001).

Cross-race and cross-gender mentoring is necessary for the mentee and the mentor to overcome negative stereotypes and develop a sense of identification with each other. Identifying and resolving complexities that may arise because of cross-race or cross-gender mentoring will help to strengthen the relationship and build a foundation that will help to provide new skills that may be beneficial for the mentee in a future role (Thomas, 2001). In situations where the mentoring relationship is being jeopardized because of cultural stereotypes, it is beneficial to provide minority mentees with a same-race (homogeneous) mentoring process. Same-race mentoring can be beneficial to minorities because there is often more psychosocial support as a result of trust and identification. Minority mentees also have an easier transition into the mentoring process, which results in a shorter initiation and professional identification early in their careers (Gonzalez-Figueroa & Young, 2005; Kogler Hill & Gant, 2000).

Diversity has become a priority for not only the corporate work environment but also in healthcare. Healthcare organizations must also respond to the high expectations from the community and the customers being served. There is a need for professional service, quality care, and innovation in order to remain competitive. Therefore, to effectively meet these expectations it is important that there are diverse experiences and qualified individuals in leadership positions to provide the best contributions so that the organization can be successful (Tourigny & Pulich, 2005).

The success of the organization depends on the leaders' ability to provide a variety of career objectives for employees regardless of their ethnicity. The position must provide a pathway to become an executive if the employee desires (Thomas, 2001). Organizations have implemented matrices to validate diversity in the company, yet embracing diversity is a slow process (Rajan & Harris, 2003; Thomas, 2001).

There have been changes in the organizational culture to improve and increase the sensitivity to diversities of employees, but these initiatives have not always been successful. Because of this, there continue to be stumbling blocks for minorities, specifically African Americans seeking career advancement within the healthcare organization (Rajan & Harris, 2003). Formal mentoring and diversity awareness programs are needed, but most importantly, making the organization appealing to minorities seeking a successful career in healthcare must be one of the organization's top priorities (Rajan & Harris, 2003).

Benefits of a Formal Mentoring Program

A formal mentoring approach provides a message to members of the organization that the executive team has given their approval. It outlines objectives with realistic expectations. The senior management team must be able to recognize the high potential employees within the group, regardless of their race or ethnicity. Strategies must be implemented to prevent turnover of African American healthcare providers (Dolan, 2004; Washington et al., 2004). Careful recruitment should be done in order to identify and employ the best and most qualified minorities.

After careful selection of qualified African Americans and other minorities for entry-level positions, attention should be given to a number of details. Promotions should reflect diversity among employees being promoted; networking groups and committees should be implemented and supported from an executive level; workshops should be led to address the discomfort among employees in regard to race; members of the executive team must participate in workshops addressing diversity; and most important, employees should be promoted based on work ethics and job performance (Shur Bilchik, 2000; Thomas, 2001). This approach will improve diversity awareness within the organization and remove potential barriers that may exclude qualified employees from being promoted.

Conclusion

The review of the literature presents information to support the fact that mentoring has been identified as an important tool for the professional advancement of employees at all levels of the organization. Newly hired employees as well as managers advance up the corporate level at a more rapid pace if they are being mentored, compared to individuals who are left alone. Minorities have been at a disadvantage in being involved in mentoring programs and often are left to learn on their own.

Additionally, the literature has also provided evidence that there is a lack of minority, specifically African American, representation at the executive levels in healthcare organizations. The need for minorities at the executive level must become a top priority for decision makers of the organization. Organizational leaders must make a commitment to not only employ African Americans and other racial minority groups but efforts must be made to implement programs providing the opportunity for these individuals to advance to the corporate level at the same rate as their Caucasian counterparts.

A review of the literature also showed that there are several reasons for the lack of mentoring for African Americans in healthcare and other organizations. Some of these reasons include the lack of cultural identification with others in the organization ("A Race Ethnicity Comparison," 2002) as well as the lack of interest of members of the executive team to take a formal approach in ensuring diversity at all levels of the organization. It is uncertain if mentoring of African Americans in healthcare can provide empowerment to improve their professional advancement.

The literature presents evidence that individuals who have been mentored have a higher average income, remain employed with the organization longer, and receive more promotions than those who have not. This qualitative case study research explored the perceived role of mentoring in the professional advancement of African American healthcare professionals to decision-making positions, and the perception of healthcare professionals regarding the importance of mentorship and empowerment in their own professional advancement. The following chapter will outlines the research design and methodology of the study as well as provides a detailed outline of the data collection and analysis, a description of the population, and an explanation of the instruments that were used for data collection.

Summary

There are several reports in the literature regarding the lack of minority representation in the healthcare industry ("A Race Ethnicity Comparison," 2002; *Bureau of Labor Statistics, 2004*; Gathers, 2003; Thomas, 2001). The resources available to quantify the number of African Americans employed in executive level positions in healthcare are limited. The available reports help to assist in validating the limited number of African Americans in decision-making positions in the healthcare industry (*Bureau of Labor Statistics, 2004*; Gathers, 2003).

Nationwide, there is a consensus that African Americans do not have equal opportunities for career advancement as compared to their Caucasian counterparts employed in the healthcare industry (Rajan & Harris, 2003; Thomas, 2001; Woog, 2005). Several factors were taken into consideration when evaluating the slow rate of advancement for African Americans to executive-level positions. Some factors included the number of minorities who are enrolled in nursing, pharmacy, and medical schools, as well as the availability of mentors for new graduates. It is equally important that members of the executive team employ strategies such as mentoring that will provide these individuals with the necessary tools for advancing their careers (Shaffer et al., 2000; Tourigny & Pulich, 2005).

Diversity in healthcare requires diversity at all levels of employment (Neil, 2003; Shaffer et al., 2000; Thomas, 2001). However, most African Americans advance more slowly in their careers than their Caucasian colleagues. High-potential Caucasians are identified early in their careers and are fast tracked to management positions. African Americans do not experience similar professional breakthrough until later in their careers, usually after they reach middle-management positions (Thomas, 2001).

Several reports have suggested that mentoring of minorities is essential to their career advancement. It is recommended that mentoring should not only be provided by individuals from the same culture but that there may be potential benefits of having cross-cultural and interracial mentoring in order to achieve a more favorable outcome for both the mentor and the mentee (Shaffer et al., 2000; Thomas, 2001; Washington et al., 2004).

CHAPTER 3: METHOD

The purpose of this qualitative case study was to explore the lived experiences of African Americans in the healthcare industry as they pertained to mentoring opportunities and their professed impact on empowerment and advancement in their careers. The participants of this study were African Americans working in hospitals or inpatient care facilities in the southeastern United States. In addition, these participants were on career paths conducive for advancement to decision-making positions. This study was conducted by using a qualitative research design. Qualitative research design provides a style of research that includes interpretive tools that help the researcher develop a database of information pertaining to the participants being observed (Yin, 1994).

Chapter 3 outlines the methodology of the study and discusses the inclusion criteria of the participants. The experiences of individuals were captured and analyzed using the basic concept of a qualitative analysis. Qualitative research methods have been used across multiple disciplines and subject matters. Additionally, the use of a qualitative research design allows several methods for collecting subjective data (Yin, 1994). For the purpose of this study, data were collected (a) through open-ended, semistructured interviews of African American decision makers in hospital and inpatient care settings and (b) through a follow up discussion utilized to assure the accuracy of the information gathered in the interview.

Research Design

A qualitative case study methodology was used to explore the lived experiences of African American hospital decision makers as related to career advancement and their perception of the role of mentorship in that process. The research design was conducted using a purposeful sampling in order to identify key African Americans in healthcare who have advanced in their careers to the highest level of the healthcare organization. The purpose of this design was to provide a sample of participants for the study who met the inclusion criteria of the study protocol.

Information was obtained through a live recorded interview regarding events that occurred in the participants' careers as healthcare professionals. A live recorded interview is considered to be an effective method of collecting information by utilizing open-ended questions. This method of data collection provided an opportunity to accurately capture the thoughts and feelings of the participants' lived experiences ("Interviews and the Philosophy," 2004; Yin, 1994).

Participants were given a copy of their transcribed interview and asked to review the document for accuracy. Additionally, each participant was asked to verify via e-mail that the interview accurately represented his or her lived experience as it pertains to mentoring and career advancement. In addition to the e-mail confirmation a follow-up telephone discussion was conducted and participants were asked if they would like to delete any comment or add any additional information to the transcribed interview. All participants stated that the interview was accurately captured and did not wish to delete or add information to the existing document.

The lived experiences of African American healthcare professionals who have not been exposed to any form of mentoring were compared to African American healthcare professionals who were mentored during their careers. The purpose was to determine whether there were common or divergent themes regarding a sense of empowerment and the ability to advance in the two groups. The exploration of these two groups' lived experiences provided substantive data to better understand the role of mentoring in the careers of African Americans healthcare professionals.

Appropriateness of Design

Qualitative research design focuses on events that happen in the natural setting. This style of research has several strategies that are designed to appropriately capture real-world data (Leedy & Ormrod, 2001). Leedy and Ormrod stated that "Qualitative researchers rarely try to simplify what they observed; instead, they recognize that the issue they are studying has many dimensions and layers" (p. 168). A case study strategy was used to investigate the phenomenon that was being explored.

Case Studies

Qualitative case study research uses research strategies that incorporate specific research approaches and methods of analysis. Case study research methods are an "empirical inquiry" (Yin, 1994, p. 13) with research questions that are designed to investigate a phenomena of real-life experiences. The use of a case study methodology for this research allowed exploration of a specific phenomenon to determine the impact of mentoring and empowerment among African American healthcare professionals. The participants' responses to the research interview questions provided detailed information regarding the lived experiences of the participants as they pertained to mentoring and professional advancement.

Qualitative Analysis

Conducting a qualitative analysis using an interview method helps to "produce a wealth of information about a much smaller number of people and cases" (Patton, 2002, p. 14). In contrast, a quantitative analysis measures the responses of individuals based on a standardized measure that allows varying responses or perspectives to "fit in a limited number of predetermined response categories to which numbers are assigned" (Patton, 2002, p. 14). The perception of healthcare professionals regarding mentoring was clearly a complex phenomenon that lent itself to qualitative analysis.

Qualitative research method provides an opportunity to gather data based on the participants lived experiences through open-ended questions. This research method was the most appropriate design for this study because it allows collection of subjective information from the participants that would be later transcribed and coded and interpreted to identify common themes (Creswell, 2004). The qualitative approach also allowed a more global exploration of the lived experiences of African Americans and their perceptions of the importance of mentoring and empowerment in their own career advancement.

Leedy and Ormrod (2001) reported that qualitative research designs allow interpretation of the data that are collected, therefore providing an opportunity to draw conclusions through interpretation of social phenomena. In a qualitative study, the individual conducting the research serves as an instrument to "gain insight about a group of individuals, develop theoretical perspectives about a pattern of behavior, and most important, identify a problem that may exist within a healthcare organization" (p. 168). Individual experiences are best captured through a qualitative approach because it allows subjective expression of feelings and emotions (Leedy & Ormrod, 2001). To be able to capture the study participants' perceptions of the role of mentoring and the effect, if any, that mentoring has had on career advancement provided the information needed to better understand the reason for the low prevalence of African American decision makers in healthcare.

Research Questions

The research questions that were answered helped to provide additional information pertaining to the impact of mentoring on career advancement in the specified population. The reason some healthcare professionals are selected to participate in a mentoring program or relationship and others are not is unknown. An individual's involvement in a mentoring program may be related to the organization's philosophy about leadership and diversity, or the individual's willingness to participate in a mentoring program.

It is also uncertain if individuals who have been mentored were selected by a member of the management team, or if they proactively sought a mentor. The research questions for this study were designed to explore the lived experiences of participants as they relate to career advancement and mentoring. Qualitative research questions are identified as central questions that are open-ended, posed in a general format, and capture information that will be answered upon completion of the study (Choudhuri, Glauser, & Peregoy, 2004). Central questions in this research were simple and provided a common theme regarding mentoring and professional advancement among the group that was being evaluated.

The participants were asked to recall information from the beginning of their professional careers in healthcare and answer a series of central questions that provided information regarding their experiences. The two broad research questions for this study were as follows:

1. What is the perceived role of mentoring in the professional advancement of African American healthcare professionals to decision-making positions?
2. What is the perception of healthcare professionals regarding the importance of mentorship and empowerment in their own professional advancement?

Population

The primary population of interest in the current study consisted of 21 male and female African American hospital or inpatient care center decision makers who were at the time working or had worked in a hospital setting located in the southeast United States during the previous 12 months. Individuals who were asked to participate in this research included healthcare leaders who had decision-making responsibilities for a hospital or department in a hospital organization. Participants were employed in a hospital with a minimum of 300 beds or may have been employed in an inpatient care facility that is affiliated with a 300 bed hospital organization.

The participants were employed in multiple healthcare organizations throughout the southeastern United States. Therefore, their place of employment was not included in the study and the names of all organizations remained anonymous. Age and years of tenure were not limiting factors for participation in this study. Healthcare professionals include nurses, pharmacists, physicians, and hospital administrators employed in a director-level position or above.

Informed Consent

The ethical treatment of all participants in this study was considered, and it was understood that the participants' rights would be protected. The participants were all leaders in their organizations and the protection of each person's opinion regarding his or her career was kept confidential. A brief explanation of the study benefits, the purpose of the study, and how the results will be shared after the study's completion were discussed with the study participants prior to the commencement of the interview (see Appendix B). Additionally, a full disclosure of the study interview questions was given to each participant prior to starting the interview.

In an effort to ensure that each study participant was aware of his or her rights and privacy, and to encourage a response to each question, each individual was provided with detailed oral and written instructions regarding the data collection process of the study (Cooper & Schindler, 2002). Participants were informed in writing of the following (see Appendix B):

1. The interview will last at least 20-30 minutes.
2. The interview will be recorded.
3. The information obtained by the participants will be kept confidential and secured without access to unauthorized individuals.
4. Participants' names and places of employment will not be used in the study to ensure privacy.
5. The data will be read by a transcriptionist, an independent data analysis contractor, the members of the research committee, and the individual responsible for conducting the research.
6. Confidentiality agreement will be signed by the transcriptionist and an authorized member of the data analysis company (see Appendix C).

After transcription, each participant received a copy of the transcribed interview to verify the accuracy of data interpretation. Participants had the opportunity to give a verbal response in person or via telephone to verify that the information in the transcript was accurate. Participants who met the inclusion criteria for participating in the study were given an informed consent. Each participant who signed the informed consent was considered to have given his or her permission to participate in the research by completing an interview using the questions outlined in Appendix D and permission to record the interview in its entirety (see Appendix B).

Sampling Frame

Participants were selected from a group of current healthcare professionals, or those who have worked in a healthcare organization within the southeastern United States during the past 12 months. These individuals included organizational leaders in nursing, medicine, pharmacy, and administration who had positions at a director's level or above. The limited number of African Americans in decision-making positions working in a healthcare organization created limitations regarding random selection of participants for this study.

The sampling method was nonrandom and participants were identified by using a referral process. Participants were selected if they met the criteria for leadership and were able to recall their professional advancement from the time they worked in an entry-level position to their current positions. Purposeful sampling expedited the process of identifying 21 African American healthcare leaders who met the inclusion criteria and solicited them for participation in the study. The sampling was terminated after data had been collected from 21 participants who consented to participate in the study.

In qualitative research studies, the interviewer seeks to obtain detailed information pertaining to the phenomenon being evaluated. The sample size helps to identify "theoretically provocative ideas" (Russell & Gregory, 2003, p. 39). Qualitative research with a large sample size may become problematic. To prevent potential problems, phenomenological studies require 10 to 50 participants (Creswell, 2004). In spite of this suggestion, there are no specific guidelines for the sample size in qualitative research. However, the sample size in a phenomenological study is usually small in order to provide in-depth information about the phenomenon being explored (Russell & Gregory, 2003).

A nonprobability purposeful sample of 21 individuals was selected to participate in this research. According to Cooper and Schindler (2002), the sample size selected should have a proportionate relationship to the population that is being evaluated. After an extensive review of the literature, it was determined that there were inadequate data available to quantify the number of healthcare decision makers employed in executive-level positions in healthcare and specifically in a hospital setting.

It is documented that African Americans represent a small percentage of the total number of healthcare executives nationwide. This group is reported to be 5% of the overall number of healthcare administrators with 1% employed at the executive level (Griffin, 2001; Hellinghausen, 2000; Woog, 2005). A sample of 21 participants was considered to be representative of the population being evaluated (Cooper & Schindler, 2002; Creswell, 2004). This qualitative research was designed to explore the specific phenomenon of mentoring and empowerment among African American healthcare professionals and to develop an in-depth understanding of the phenomenon being explored. Due to the low prevalence of African American healthcare executives and the lack of data to verify the size of the population being evaluated, 21 participants were selected as an appropriate number to adequately represent the population in this study.

Furthermore, a sample of 21 was within the range of 10-50, the number of participants recommended for a phenomenological study (Creswell, 2003). Additionally, 21 participants allowed for several responses from members of the healthcare disciplines who were included in this research. Study participants' selection was limited to the southeastern region of the United States. This geographical area was chosen because of the sizes of the states and their metropolitan cities that may have a high number of African American healthcare decision makers.

African American hospital decision makers were identified using a referral process. This referral process is known as a snowball method of population sampling. This process involves identifying an initial group of participants that are representative of the population. This initial population refers another subgroup that is representative of the population (Heckathorn, 2002). Requests for participation were made by e-mailing an introductory letter to potential participants to request participation in the study, and to provide a brief overview of the study and the study population (see Appendix A). The initial group of study participants was selected from a group of decision makers who are professional colleagues of the study investigator.

The sample included managers with decision-making responsibilities who met the previous criteria, directors of healthcare departments, and other members of the executive team. Each participant (a) met the inclusion criteria; (b) was currently employed in a decision-making position and (c) was employed in a hospital with at least 300 beds, or an inpatient care facility affiliated with a hospital. Nondecision makers were not to be included in the sample to avoid the inclusion of entry-level managers who may not have been working in a position in which they were capable of contributing to the decisions that influence the daily operation of the organization. Additionally, decision makers who were not then employed in an inpatient care setting or may not have been employed in such a setting during the previous 12 months were also excluded.

These exclusions allowed accurate data from individuals who were key decision makers who could provide the most accurate recollections of their lived experiences in healthcare. The inclusion criteria for the study participants were as follows:

1. African American healthcare worker.
2. Employee in decision-making position within a hospital or inpatient care setting during the previous 12 months.
3. Have direct reports or have decision-making responsibilities for the daily operation of a department or hospital.
4. Employees whose position in the healthcare organization is at a director's level or above.
5. Male or female.
6. Willing to participate in a live interview.
7. Willing to share career experiences.
8. Willing to sign an informed consent form for participating in the study.
9. Employed in a hospital or inpatient care facility that is located within the southeastern United States.

Confidentiality

Confidentiality of information obtained from study participants is important when conducting research. Privacy laws are strictly enforced, and each participant's right to privacy and confidentiality was honored (Cooper & Schindler, 2002). The privacy and confidentiality of information collected from these decision makers were kept in the strictest confidence, and each individual's right to privacy held in the highest regard. The data were presented in a manner that kept each individual's response and participation anonymous (Leedy & Ormrod, 2001).

The interview did not include any identifiers that could disclose the individuals' names, places of employment, or their employers. Each study participant was assigned a number according to the order in which his or her informed consent was received. After completion of the interview, the recording of the interview was stored in a locked file cabinet in an office. Access to the file cabinet was limited to the individual responsible for conducting the study.

The responses were reviewed by the research investigator, a transcriptionist, a third party individual who analyzed the data, and the members of the research committee. Both the transcriptionist and a representative of the company that analyzed the data were required to sign a confidentiality agreement. Additionally, these individuals were required to return all printed and recorded research documents to the individual conducting the study within seven business days after the completion of the study.

There were no identifiers that disclosed the identity of the participants to anyone except the person conducting the interview. The responses of all 21 participants were compiled and reported based on themes developed from the interviews without any identifying information. These documents will be kept for 3 years in the same locked file cabinet with the other research documents.

Following the completion of this research, the identifying information will be kept for 3 years and after that time all recordings will be destroyed. All informed consents, confidentiality agreements, and interview transcriptions will be shredded after 3 years using a cross shredder. This will prevent the possibility of identifying any information included in the documents. The tape cassette recording will be destroyed by opening the cassette and unraveling the tape strip, after which the tape strip will be cut into smaller pieces.

Geographic Location

The study was conducted in the southeastern United States. The participants were employed in a hospital organization or an inpatient care organization affiliated with a hospital organization within this geographical location. The healthcare organizations that were considered for selection of participants were moderate to large organizations with at least 300 inpatient beds.

Instrumentation

The study interviews were completed in person when possible. Study participants who were unable to meet in person to participate in the interviews had the option to participate in the study via telephone. The data were collected by recording the response of each study participant and then transcribed after completion of the interview.

The study interview questions were designed to solicit open-ended responses and provide details regarding the lived experiences in career achievement of African Americans in healthcare who have been mentored at various stages in their career as well as those who had not. Participants who completed the interview via telephone received an electronic copy of the informed consent and were required to sign and return the consent prior to participating in the interview. The signed consents were mailed to the study investigator's home. The return address was listed on the consent.

Collecting data through an interview process requires an organized approach in order to identify a pattern in the response to each question. Posing open-ended questions also provides the opportunity for each respondent to provide detailed responses to the questions being asked (Yin, 1994). This method of data collection provided the opportunity to identify patterns in the career experiences of the respondents.

The instrument that was used in this study consisted of open-ended questions in order to solicit in-depth responses (see Appendix D). A pilot study was conducted utilizing three individuals who were representative of the study population to determine the face validity of the survey interview questions, and to assure that the questions were understandable and unbiased. Based on the responses elicited in the pilot study, appropriate modifications were made to the questions.

The interview questions provided subjective recall information from each participant. The questions were sequenced to stimulate interest in career achievement, with queries pertaining to mentoring deferred toward the end of the interview. According to Cooper and Schindler (2002), question sequencing is significant in determining how successful the instrument will be. It is recommended that the most stimulating questions are asked at the beginning of the interview to prevent bias from the participants regarding organizational support of their careers.

Data Collection

This method of data collection was conducted primarily through direct contact with each participant and was in the form of a tape recorded interview (Meltzoff, 2003). This research was completed by using open-ended questions to interview 21 African American healthcare decision makers. Each participant provided answers to a series of questions that are outlined in Appendix D.

After identifying individuals who had met the inclusion criteria for the research, the identified individuals were contacted via telephone or e-mail and provided with an overview of the research. If they agreed to participate, an appointment was scheduled to conduct the study interview. Participants who had consented to participate in this study were required to sign a written consent giving permission to collect information and record the responses to a series of questions that had been validated from a pilot study of a similar group. Permission was obtained from study participants to authorize a taped version of the interview, which was evaluated after all the data had been collected from all study participants.

A handheld tape recorder was used to collect live responses to the study interview. The data were collected by conducting the interview in person with the study participants. In situations where it was not feasible to conduct the interview in person, an electronic informed consent was sent to the study participants. After receiving permission from the study participant to participate in the study, the interview was conducted in person or via telephone and the study participants' responses to the interview were recorded.

The interviews were recorded using a Radio Shack ® micro-cassette and phone recorder model TRC 300. Upon completion of the data collection of the participants' responses to the study interview, the data were analyzed. After completion of data collection and analysis, the tape recordings were stored in a locked safety box that was placed in a file cabinet. An additional copy of the recordings was stored on a compact disc, which was kept in a separate locked file cabinet at the same location. All documentation and recordings will be stored for 3 years past the completion of the study.

Interviews in a qualitative study should be designed to permit exploration of the topic. Open-ended questions will encourage the participants to expand their answers (Salkind, 2003). Upon completion of the data collection, participants' responses were divided into two groups - those who were mentored during their professional careers in healthcare and those who were not. This allowed comparison of the lived experiences of those participants who were mentored with those who were not in terms of common and divergent themes.

To assure that the data were an accurate representation of the lived experiences of the participants, a second follow-up discussion was scheduled with each participant to verify the interpreted data. The second follow-up was conducted via telephone or via e-mail. During the second meeting, each participant was informed of the interpretation of his or her lived experience. The purpose of the second follow-up was to allow participants to comment on the results of the analysis in order to assure that the results were an accurate depiction of their lived experiences. Each participant's signature on the informed consent was considered as consent to have the responses recorded during the initial collection of data, and for follow-up verification of the data.

Data Analysis

To reduce bias, the audiotape interviews were transcribed by an independent transcriptionist into a Microsoft Word document for further analysis. The analysis was completed by a professional data analysis company and the initial stage of analysis consisted of reading the interview text and developing preliminary themes based on the model outlined in the modified van Kaam data analysis (Moustakas, 1994). Moustakas' methodology consists of four steps: horizontalization, invariant constituents, thematic patterns, and compatible invariant constituents.

Using Moustakas' methodology, the interview text is compiled and irrelevant and redundant text is eliminated. After which thematic patterns are identified and coded to identify invariant constituents and compatible invariant constituents among the interviews. After the data are coded and themes are identified, the results are compiled and presented as they relate to the research questions.

This method of analysis provides insight and better understanding of the phenomenon that is being explored. In a modified van Kaam study analysis method, invariant constituents are identified and validated, and then a composite of each participant's experience is created and combined with the experiences of all the other participants to represent a general theme that describes the lived experiences of all participants in the group (Moustakas, 1994).

Identifying common themes such as the impact of mentors on professional growth, timeline of professional career in which mentoring was initiated, length of the mentoring process, and level of management in which mentoring was employed were determined by content analysis. Following the development of the themes, all interviews were coded as to the presence or absence of the themes. The data were analyzed to identify themes in mentoring and professional advancement as well as the impact of mentoring in empowering African American healthcare professionals. Differences and similarities in themes of African- Americans who have been mentored and those who have not were also analyzed.

Validity

Testing of instruments for validity assures that the instrument being used can accurately measure or test what is intended. The importance of having a valid instrument is to ensure that any differences seen in the group being tested are a true representation of the group and can be generalized across a similar group in a similar setting (Cooper & Schindler, 2002; Creswell, 2003). The interview instrument that was used to collect data in this study consisted of a series of open-ended interview questions (see Appendix D). The interview instrument was developed using a series of open-ended questions designed to gather information based on the lived experiences of the participants. This instrument was designed to provide the participants with the opportunity to provide an accurate recall of their perceptions of situations pertaining to their careers in healthcare.

The questions in the study interview had not been used previously and were validated by a small pilot group of three individuals who were representative of the group to be tested. After completion of the pilot interview, the responses were evaluated to determine whether the questions were written in a format that provided the same interpretation to each of the three members of the sample group. The purpose of this pilot study was to provide face validity by determining commonality in interpretation of the questions, to determine if the responses to the questions provided sufficient data to answer the research questions, and also to determine the length of time needed for the interview.

After completing, collecting, and evaluating the responses from the sample group, the validity of the interview questions was determined by the above-mentioned evaluation process. Changes were made to the interview questions to accurately capture the required information to satisfy the purpose of the study. The validity of the questions was important to ensure that the data collected were an accurate representation of the lived experiences of the African American population being studied.

Summary

Chapter 3 outlined the study design, methodology, validity, description of the instrument, data collection process, and a description of the participants. Subjective recall data from study participants were collected and evaluated to provide new information regarding their perception of the impact of mentoring for African Americans working in leadership positions in hospital organizations and inpatient care centers. Chapter 4 outlines the implementation of the research, and presents the research findings of the study as they relate to the research questions.

CHAPTER 4: RESULTS

The purpose of this qualitative case study was to provide a better understanding of the role of mentorship in advancing the careers of African American healthcare administrators and executives through exploration of their lived experiences as they relate to mentoring as well as perceived difficulties in advancing to executive positions within their careers. In order to better understand the role of mentoring in professional advancement, it is important to explore the perceptions of professionals who have and those who have not been mentored during their careers. The research questions of the current study were as follows:

1. What is the perceived role of mentoring in the professional advancement of African American healthcare professionals to decision-making positions?
2. What is the perception of healthcare professionals regarding the importance of mentorship and empowerment in their own professional advancement?

The Moustakas' (1994) modification of the van Kaam method of qualitative analysis was used in this study. Moustakas' methodology consists of four steps: horizontalization, invariant constituents, thematic patterns, and compatible invariant constituents. *Horizontalization* is the term used to refer to the actual interview responses for each participant. The invariant constituents are the text that remains after initial reduction of the interview text to remove irrelevant text and redundant responses. Thematic patterns are those portions of the invariant constituents that are repeated in various contexts, and compatible invariant constituents are the reliable patterns that occur from one interviewee to the next.

The purpose of the current chapter is to present the findings of this study as they relate to the two research questions. Initially, the demographic, organizational, and employment characteristics of the interviewees are presented. The professional aspirations and job satisfaction of the respondents are then described. The main section of the results begins with the respondents' understanding/definitions of mentoring, and an analysis of the role of each participant's personal mentor. An analysis of the participants' perceptions of the importance of mentoring follows, and the chapter ends with a summary.

Validity of Instrument

Face validity of the instrument was determined by conducting a pilot study with three individuals who were representative of the population. These individuals were interviewed in a setting of their choice to provide comfort. The interviews were conducted in person or via telephone conference. The participants were given the opportunity to validate the transcribed audio responses of the study questions.

Pilot Study

The interview questions were designed to explore the importance or lack of importance of mentoring on professional advancement based on the lived experiences of African American healthcare professionals. Twenty-one questions were created to solicit responses from an initial group of three research participants. Each pilot participant was asked a series of demographic questions in addition to the interview questions (see Appendix E).

The questions used in the study were not used previously for research or in this population. A series of 21 questions (see Appendix E) were used to conduct an open-ended semistructured interview. The questions were tested for face validity using three individuals that were representative of the population.

Each participant's response was recorded using a handheld micro-cassette recorder. The responses were later transcribed and each individual was given the opportunity to validate the accuracy of their responses by reviewing the transcribed interview. Each response to the 21 questions was evaluated to determine (a) accuracy of interpretation, (b) similar responses to different questions, and (c) wording of questions to solicit an in-depth response.

After reviewing each of the three interviews, changes were made to some of the questions according to the responses of each of prestudy participant. Question 15 was reworded to determine the importance of a mentor in providing networking opportunities with members of upper level management. Question 16, 17, and 21 were deleted. Question 18 was reworded to determine how long it took the participant to get to their current position (see Appendix E).

Interview Process

A series of predetermined questions (see Appendix D) were used to interview a sample of 21 individuals who were purposely selected. These individual were employed in a hospital organization in the southeastern United States and were considered to be decision makers. An initial group of participants was identified by the research investigator and a snowball method of sampling was used to identify other potential participants.

Additional participants were contacted via telephone and e-mail. An overview of the study was given to each potential participant verbally if contacted via telephone and via e-mail if contacted electronically. This method of sampling was considered to be most effective because of the limited number of African American hospital decision makers which made this group a hard to reach population. Prior to the commencement of the interview, each participant was given the opportunity to ask questions about the details of the study and his or her expectation as a study participant.

After each participant consented to participate in the study, each participant agreed upon a time and place that was most convenient for him or her to conduct the study interview. The interview was conducted in an informal manner with the participant responding to a series of 18 open-ended questions. The questions were developed to obtain a description of the participants' lived experiences as they pertain to mentoring and professional advancement. Each participant's interview was recorded and a transcript of the interview was provided to the participant for verification of the accuracy of the transcribed interview.

Organizational, Demographic, and Employment Characteristics of Sample

Characteristics of the Organization

Table 1 (see Appendix F) presents a summary of the key characteristics of the organizations where each interviewee was employed. For the number of beds in the organization, responses ranged from 40 where the main institution had a total of over 1,000 beds (indicated by a participant whose department was primarily an outpatient facility) to 3,300. Some of the participants characterized the size of their department in terms of the number of employees, while others described it in terms of the number of visits or patients seen per year. The varying responses to the size of the department were a result of the various disciplines of the participants. Some participants were employed in an administrative department while others were clinicians and were employed in departments where both the number of employees and the number of patient beds determined the size of the department.

The number of employees in the participants' department ranged from 6 to 350, while the number of annual patients/visits ranged from 28,000 to 100,000. The number of direct reports required of the participants ranged from 0 to 65. As would be expected, the interviewees came from a range of organizations and departments with highly variable structures (e.g., inpatient versus outpatient facilities, physician-only departments versus other types, etc.), and therefore the current sample contained a broad range of participants.

Demographic Characteristics of the Sample

The demographic characteristics of the sample (age, education, and whether or not they described having a mentor) are provided in Table 2 (see Appendix F). Of the 21 interviewees, 19 stated that they had been mentored in their careers while 2 indicated that they had not. The focus of the analysis was on the 19 individuals who reported having a mentor, with the data from the 2 individuals without a mentor being used to supplement the main results.

The ages of the interviewees ranged from 41 to 62 ($M = 50.50$, $SD = 6.26$). There were a variety of educational degrees for the sample, with the most common being Doctors of Pharmacy ($n = 6$, 28.6%), Nursing degrees ($n = 5$, 23.8%), Medical Doctors ($n = 4$, 19%), Master's in Business Administration ($n = 3$, 14.3%), Bachelor's of Pharmacy ($n = 2$, 9.5%), and Master's in Social Work ($n = 1$, 4.8%).

Employment Characteristics of the Sample

The employment characteristics of the sample are shown in Table 3 (see Appendix F), including current position, years working in the healthcare field, and years with the current organization. Current positions were highly variable, with the most common being Director of Pharmacy (*n* = 6, 28.6%). All participants were in some form of supervisory role. The number of years working in healthcare ranged from 4 to 38 (*M* = 24.25, *SD* = 8.16), and the number of years working within the current organization ranged from less than a year to 27 years (*M* = 13.05, *SD* = 9.41).

Professional Goals, Professional Development, and Job Satisfaction

Table 4 (see Appendix F) provides summary information related to professional goals, professional development, and job satisfaction. Of the mentored interviewees, 13 (68.4%) indicated that they were satisfied, while three (15.8%) stated that they were very satisfied (Participant 2, 10, & 19), three (15.8%) stated that they were somewhat satisfied (either "pretty satisfied" (Participant 6), "80% satisfied" (Participant 7), or "yes" and "no" (Participant 9), and one (5.3%) was not satisfied (Participant 13). Ten (52.6%) of the mentored respondents stated that their current position was the one to which they aspired (Participant, 1, 4, 9, 10, 12, 13, 16, 17, 19, & 21).

Reasons for aspiring only to the current position included a desire for a balanced life (e.g., "too much responsibility [in a higher position]" (Participant 2), the closeness of retirement, and organizational structures (e.g., "in our organization structure. . . this is the highest position [in nursing]" (Participant 21). Among the nine (47.4%) mentored individuals who aspired to a higher position (Participant 1, 3, 6, 8, 12, 17, 19, 20, & 21), the main reason was good job performance (e.g., "performance as a leader" (Participant 12), and "because I'm very competent" (Participant 22).

Other mentored individuals who desired a higher position noted that they did not want to go even higher primarily because of time constraints related to retirement (e.g., "I may reach the target [retirement] age before I can achieve that" (Participant 7), and a dislike of organizational politics. One individual who aspired for a higher position noted, "I don't think they're going to give someone Black a . . . chairmanship of a department" (Participant 17).

While both nonmentored interviewees (Participants 1 & 8) stated that they were satisfied with their jobs, they were far from their career goals, with one stating that "career goals expand far beyond this" (Participant 8), while the other noted, "I'm still not at the top yet" (Participant 1).

Both of the nonmentored individuals aspired to a higher position (e.g., "[I need to] build up more time and get to understand the bureaucracy and the policies within the organization" (Participant 8), although one noted a desire to have a balanced personal and professional life.

Data Collection

Data collection was conducted primarily through direct contact with each participant and was in the form of a tape recorded interview (Meltzoff, 2003). Each participant provided answers to a series of questions that are outlined in Appendix D. A handheld tape recorder was used to collect live responses to the study interview. The data were collected by conducting the interview in person ($n = 6$, 28.6%) and via telephone ($n = 15$, 71.4%) with the study participants. In situations where it was not feasible to conduct the interview in person, an informed consent was mailed or faxed to the study participant. After receiving permission from each participant to participate in the study, the interviews were conducted via telephone (*n* = 15, 71.4%) or in person (*n* = 6, 28.6%) and the study participants' responses to the interview were recorded.

Participants whose interviews were conducted in person chose the time and location that were most convenient for them. Telephone interviews were also scheduled at the convenience of the participant. Prior to starting the interview, participants were given a copy of the interview questions, which included a definition of mentoring (see Appendix D).

For the purpose of continuity and to prevent extraneous information that did not directly pertain to the study questions that were being asked, participants were given the opportunity at the end of the interview to provide additional information that they thought was important or pertinent to the questions previously asked. At the end of the interview, participants were also reminded that they would be provided with a transcript of their interview and verification of the transcript would be completed during a follow-up to the interview. The interview was recorded using a Radio Shack ® micro-cassette and phone recorder model TRC 300. Upon completion of the data collection of the participants' responses to the study interview, the data were transcribed and analyzed.

Interviews in a qualitative study should be designed to permit exploration of the topic. Open-ended questions encouraged the participants to expand their answers (Salkind, 2003). Upon completion of the data collection, participants' responses were divided into two groups, those who were mentored during their professional career in healthcare (*N* = 19, 90.5%) and those who were not (*N* = 2, 9.5%). This allowed comparison of the lived experiences of those participants who were mentored with those who were not in terms of common and divergent themes.

To assure that the data were an accurate representation of the lived experiences of the participants, a follow-up discussion was scheduled with each participant to verify the interpreted data. The second follow-up was conducted after the interview via telephone to verify that the responses to the study questions were accurately captured and transcribed. The purpose of the follow-up discussion was to allow participants to comment on the results of the analysis in order to assure that the results were an accurate depiction of their lived experiences.

Data Analysis

To reduce bias, the audiotape interviews were transcribed by an independent transcriptionist into a Microsoft Word document for further analysis. The analysis of the transcribed interviews was completed by a professional data analysis company, and the initial stage of analysis consisted of reading the interview text and developing preliminary themes based on the model outlined in the modified van Kaam data analysis (Moustakas, 1994). This method of analysis provides insight and better understanding of the phenomenon that is being explored. Identifying common themes such as the impact of mentors on professional growth and the timeline for which mentoring was initiated during his or her career was accomplished by content analysis. Following the development of the themes, all interviews were coded to identify themes.

Findings

The Role of a Mentor

The first research question of this study was as follows: *What is the perceived role of mentoring in the professional advancement of African American healthcare professionals to decision-making positions*? The results begins with a discussion of the participants' explicit definitions and understanding of mentoring and the mentoring process in general, based on responses to the prompt, *please give me your definition of mentoring*. From these explicit definitions, preliminary aspects of the role of a mentor were developed.

Explicit and General Definitions of Mentoring

Some participants provided extended definitions and related the role of a mentor to their own experiences, while others provided brief, somewhat general definitions (Table 5, see Appendix F). Fagenson and Amendola (1993) defined a mentor as follows:

> An experienced, influential member of an organization who provides career guidance and psychosocial support to a less experienced organizational member. Mentors serve as role models and provide protégés with their time, support, direction, and feedback regarding career plans, actions and interpersonal development (p. 58).

The definitions of mentoring provided by the respondents in the current study overlap considerably with the definition provided by Fagenson and Amendola.

Preliminary Roles of a Mentor From Explicit but General Definitions

Table 6 (see Appendix F) presents the five preliminary roles/characteristics (the comparable invariate constituents) of a mentor derived from the participants' explicit definitions of mentoring. The five most frequently mentioned characteristics of a mentor were (a) someone who has professional experience, (b) someone who is a good listener, (c) someone with whom you establish a personal relationship, (d) someone who sets an example or serves as a role model, and (e) someone who helps bring out your best and achieve your goals. The most frequently mentioned role/characteristic of a mentor was someone who brings out your best or helps you to achieve your goals, which was mentioned by 9 (42.9%) of the 21 respondents (including both of those who indicated that they did not have a mentor). Respondents noted that a mentor is "Someone who helps you set goals and objectives, helps you get there in reaching those goals and objectives" (Participant 1), someone "who can share insight and provide specific guidance on how to achieve goals" (Participant 9), and someone who shows you the "things that you can do" (Participant 2).

The next most-mentioned characteristic of a mentor is someone who has relevant professional experience, which 8 (38.1%) of the 21 interviewees mentioned in their definition of mentoring (including 1 of the 2 interviewees who did not have a mentor). For example, respondents noted that a mentor is "someone with professional experience that you are trying to acquire" (Participant 5), "someone in a leadership position that has experience in a particular area where you'd like to go" (Participant 12), and "someone that had attained certain things that I was aspiring to" (Participant 21).

Six (28.6%) of the respondents mentioned the personal nature of the mentor/mentee relationship (including one of the two respondents without a mentor). The interviewees described a mentor as "a big brother, a father, a teacher, a counselor, coach"

(Participant 8), and noted that mentoring "is taking someone under your wing" (Participant 6). Another respondent stated that

> Mentoring to me is very personal. Some people look at it as possibly a way to just have someone you can call upon but in order to be effective you have to be able to expose your weaknesses and your strengths as well (Participant 7).

One respondent expanded on the personal nature of the mentoring relationship, stating "A mentor is someone who can advise you on your career and sometimes on your personal [and] professional [lives] . . . sort of how they relate to each other at any given point in your career" (Participant 15).

Five of the respondents (23.8%) mentioned that the mentor was someone you could talk to, someone who was a good listener (neither of those who did not have a mentor were in this group). To these interviewees, a mentor was someone "you can talk to about where you are" (Participant 3), and "Someone who provides a listening ear and serves as a sounding board for my ideas my thoughts, any issues or problems" (Participant 22). Finally, five of the respondents (23.8%) described the mentor as a role model, or someone who sets an example (neither of those who did not have a mentor were in this group). A mentor was described as someone who could "be an example" (Participant 10). One respondent, after a long definition of what a mentor was, summarized by stating "a role model" (Participant 7).

In summary, the preliminary roles and characteristics of a mentor were derived from the participants' explicit definition of mentoring, that is, their responses when directly asked what mentoring is. Five roles/characteristics of a mentor were mentioned by at least 5 of the 21 respondents. A mentor was described as someone who "help them to achieve their best" (Participant 8), "someone who has professional experience in a particular area" (Participant 12), "teaching someone the ropes, helping them to navigate their professional field so that they too can be successful in whatever area that they chose to go" (Participant 19), "someone who is a good listener" (Participant 22), and "someone who sets an example or serves as a role model" (Participant 7).

Final Analysis of the Role of a Mentor From Personal Mentor Roles

As noted above, the preliminary set of roles that a mentor is expected to fulfill was taken from the participants' explicit responses to the interview prompt *Please give me your definition of mentoring*. The preliminary roles (invariant constituents) defined above apply to the participants' perceptions of mentors in general. In another section of the interviews, the participants were asked specifically about the role of their own mentor.

Beyond the general question about a definition of a mentor, this section consisted of modifications and additions to the preliminary roles of a mentor described above. In addition, the purpose of this section was to take information from the interviews as a whole in order to develop a final set of mentor roles. Table 7 presents a summary of the participants' responses to the interview question I*n regard to the person that you mentioned previously, what was their specific role?* As can be seen from this table, each of the preliminary roles outlined above appeared in terms of the personal mentor roles.

In addition, one additional role was defined: problem solver. Eight of the 19 interviewees who reported having a mentor (42.1%) mentioned some aspect of the mentor as a problem solver in responses to this question. Typical responses included that the mentor "answered questions for me when I needed help" (Participant 4), and "When I had problems, for instance professional problems, I could call and get their opinion" (Participant 5). Additional responses included the mentor provided information "how best to handle the specific situation" (Participant 17), and "if I had an issue with a person or an organization or direction or strategy she would sort of put things in perspective for me" (Participant 22).

In summary, one additional mentor role (invariant constituent) was added based on the participants' responses to the question about their personal mentor: problem solver. The final six mentor roles defined in the analysis for the first research question are (a) someone who has professional experience, (b) someone who is a good listener, (c) someone with whom you establish a personal relationship, (d) someone who sets an example or serves as a role model, (e) someone who helps bring out your best and achieve your goals, and (f) someone who assists in solving specific problems.

The Importance of Mentorship

The second research question of this study was W*hat is the perception of healthcare professionals regarding the importance of mentorship and empowerment in their own professional advancement*? Only the 19 individuals who indicated that they had a mentor were relevant to this examination. Participants 1 and 6 both reported that they did not have a mentor or someone who helps to guide their professional career. These individuals both stated that mentoring might be important but could not provide subjective information on the relationship between mentoring and empowerment.

Information regarding the participants' perceptions of the importance of mentoring was derived from various sections of the interviews. Table 8 presents a summary of the participants' perceptions of the importance of a mentor, along with relevant quotations and information on whether the mentor was of the same gender and/or race as the interviewee. Overall, 11 of the 19 participants with a mentor (57.9%) indicated that they felt that the mentor was very important, while 4 (21.1%) felt that the mentor was important and 4 (21.1%) felt that mentor was potentially important. Among those who felt that the mentor was very important, representative responses include "most definitely" (Participant 1), "absolutely helpful" (Participant 14), "very helpful" (Participant 20), and mentoring is "an excellent tool" (Participant 4).

Further analysis of the responses of the participants who were mentored (90.4%, *n* = 19) revealed that they have achieved their professional goals or are pleased with their career accomplishments (84.2%, *n* = 16). In contrast, participants who were not mentored felt that they have not achieved their professional goals (Participant 6) or have not achieved their professional goals but were pleased with the progress of their career (Participant 1). Participants who were mentored felt that mentoring was important and can possibly be the conduit in getting to the next level of their professional careers. Participant 1 stated that, "If there was a structured mentorship or mentor program of which these aspiring (especially the young kids coming in) can tap into they would have knowledge and camaraderie," The participant went on to say,

> Yes I believe that African Americans need a mentor to help them to get to the next level of management. They need someone to help them to get into the inner circle. There are politics and cliques and without someone to take them and help them along the way, they may become discouraged and lost along the way (Participant 1).

For those who felt that mentoring was important but not very important, one stated,

> I believe that mentoring provides the tools necessary . . . not to say that it's impossible [without mentoring] but it becomes much better for you to have someone that you can call upon that can help you to give you those strengths you need to get to where you want to go (Participant 7).

Those who were categorized as responding that mentoring was potentially important usually had an important qualification to their response, such as

> I think the process, depending on who the person is, yes, would give you an opportunity to prepare you for other types of positions but there are a lot of factors that actually determine whether that is effective or not (Participant 11).

Gender/Racial Similarity of Mentor/Mentee

One interesting aspect of the current study was that the interviewees were asked if their mentor had the same gender and/or the same racial background as the interviewee. This information is provided along with the quotations about the importance of mentoring in Table 8. Overall, there did not appear to be a relationship between the demographic (gender and race) similarity of the mentor and the mentee on the one hand, and the perceptions of the importance of mentoring on the other hand.

For example, those who had the same gender but a different race as their mentor had the following frequencies: potentially important, 1; important, 1; very important, 2. Those who had a different gender but the same race as their mentor had the following frequencies: potentially important, 1; important, 0; very important, 4. Those who had the same gender and race had the following frequencies: potentially important, 0, important,

2; very important, 2. While broad generalizations are not possible with the current sample size (and the present study was not designed to test a hypothesis about the relationship between perceptions of mentoring and gender/racial similarity), the distribution of responses indicates that an individual's perception of the importance of mentoring does not depend heavily on whether or not the mentor had the same gender or race as the mentee.

Summary

The purpose of this qualitative case study was to provide a better understanding of the role of mentorship in advancing the careers of African American healthcare administrators and executives through exploration of their lived experiences as they relate to mentoring as well as perceived difficulties in advancing to executive positions within their careers. The first research question was *What is the perceived role of mentoring in the professional advancement of African American healthcare professionals to decision-making positions*? The most commonly mentioned role for a mentor was someone who brings out one's best which in turn assists in achieving goals.

This aspect of mentorship was related to the functional aspects of the mentor/mentee relationship in that it is very goal-oriented. The second theme was related to problem solving. Respondents indicated that a mentor was someone that one could go to with a specific problem or issue in order to get the guidance needed to overcome the obstacle.

The second most-mentioned characteristic of a mentor is someone who has relevant professional experience. Thus, respondents felt that it was important that the mentor was someone similar to themselves who had been down the road that they were currently on. The fourth theme related to the personal nature of the mentor/mentee relationship. Respondents felt that the mentor/mentee was personal in addition to professional, and that the mentor would act as an emotionally involved guide through the mentee's professional life.

The fifth theme was that a mentor was a good listener. Specifically, a mentor was seen as someone who, in addition to providing guidance, would provide the important service of allowing the mentee to speak his or her mind openly. The final theme was related to the mentor being a role model for the mentee. A mentor was seen as someone who could be emulated by the mentee. In summary, six mentor roles were defined in the interviews. Mentors were described as (a) someone who helps bring out one's best which in turn assists in achieving goals, (b) someone who assists in problem solving, (c) someone who has professional experience in a relevant area, (d) someone with whom you establishes a personal relationship, (e) someone who is a good listener, and (f) someone who sets an example or serves as a role model.

The second research question of this study asked *What is the perception of healthcare professionals regarding the importance of mentorship and empowerment in their own professional advancement*? It was clear from the interviews that the respondents placed a high value on mentorship. Respondents either indicated that mentors were very important (57.9%), important (21.1%), or at the very least potentially important (21.1%).

None of the respondents indicated that they did not feel that mentors were, or could be, important. Those who felt that the mentor was only potentially important tended to emphasize that a mentor had to be involved and concerned to be of benefit to the mentee, and that merely having a designated mentor was not enough for it to be helpful to the mentee. In addition, a more detailed analysis indicated that there does not appear to be a relationship between the demographic (gender and race) similarity of the mentor and the mentee on the one hand, and the perceptions of the importance of mentoring on the other hand. Chapter 5 discusses the summary, recommendations, and conclusions of the study.

CHAPTER 5: SUMMARY, RECOMMENDATIONS, AND CONCLUSIONS

This chapter presents the conclusions drawn from the review of the literature, the methodology, and the analysis of the data in the summary. Interpretation and evaluation of the findings and the significance of the study to leadership will be presented in the conclusion. Additionally, the significance of the study and the significance of the study to leadership and recommendations for further research will also be presented.

Purpose of the Study

The purpose of this qualitative case study was to explore the lived experiences of African Americans in the healthcare industry as they pertained to mentoring opportunities and their professed impact on empowerment and advancement in their careers. The 21 participants of this study were African Americans working in hospitals or inpatient care facilities in the southeastern United States and were on a career path that is conducive for advancement to a decision-making position. The role of a mentor was explored through the lived experiences of the participants as they relate to mentoring and the perceived benefits if any of mentoring and empowerment.

Mentoring began as an informal process where experienced individuals often times senior executives, would identify a less experienced employee that reminded them of themselves and take the initiative to groom them. As mentoring became a more frequent process, the grooming and development of these less experienced individuals started to take place outside of the work place in places such as the golf course. These gatherings consist of members of the *good old boy* network which is considered to be an elite group of influential Caucasian men who are socially connected and usually this network does not include minorities or anyone who is not a part of this elite group (Jenkins, 2005).

As the number of African Americans continues to increase in healthcare, the need for professional guidance becomes necessary to provide networking opportunities, professional guidance, and empowerment. A formal support system has been shown to be beneficial to help motivate and help fast track the careers of African Americans as is seen in promising Caucasians (Jenkins, 2005; Thomas, 2001). Studies pertaining to mentoring that have received attention have primarily evaluated healthcare executives. Additional insight is needed to evaluate organizational leaders in a hospital in the areas of nursing, administration, medicine, and pharmacy ("A Race Ethnicity Comparison," 2002).

The following research questions were answered by this study: What is the perceived role of mentoring in the professional advancement of African American healthcare professionals to decision-making positions? And, what is the perception of healthcare professionals regarding the importance of mentorship and empowerment in their own professional advancement?

According to the literature, it was believed that mentoring plays an important role in professional advancement and therefore, having a mentor during the early years of one's career might provide professional guidance and empowerment to advance more quickly to a decision-making position (Dancer, 2003; Larson, 2006; Tourigny & Pulich, 2005). For the purpose of this study, a semicontrolled interview format was used to provide an opportunity to ask open-ended questions to gain insight about events that occurred in the participants' professional careers (Yin, 1994). Participants were asked to recall information from the beginning of their professional careers in healthcare and answer a series of central questions (see Appendix D) that provided information regarding their experiences.

Even though each person's experience and interpretation of a common situation may be different, by asking each participant the same questions in the same format and coding the response to identify common themes, it was possible to identify similarities in the experiences of the participants. Data were gathered using an informal interview process through an open-ended question, semistructured interview. The questions focused on the role of mentoring in the participants' careers, and the perceived impact of mentoring on their professional development as well as the perceived impact if any of mentoring on empowerment. A modified van Kaam (Moustakas, 1994) method of analysis was used to analyze the interviews from the 21 participants who responded to the 18 item interview questions (see Appendix D). A modified van Kaam methodology consists of four steps: horizontalization, invariant constituents, thematic patterns, and compatible invariant constituents. A composite of the responses was developed and common themes were identified using the method that was described in Chapter 4.

Summary

The study started with the participants' response to 18 open-ended questions (see Appendix D) that were driven by two broad research questions. Six themes were identified for the first research question that defined the role of mentoring in professional advancement. Mentors were described as (a) someone who helps bring out your one's best which in turn assists in achieving goals, (b) someone who assists in problem solving, (c) someone who has professional experience in a relevant area, (d) someone with whom one establishes a personal relationship, (e) someone who is a good listener, and (f) someone who sets an example or serves as a role model.

The responses to the second research question that explored the participants' perception of mentorship on empowerment and career advancement revealed that respondents believed that mentoring was a valuable tool. It was clear from the interviews that the respondents placed a high value on mentorship. Respondents either indicated that mentors were very important (57.9%), important (21.1%), or at the very least potentially important (21.1%). A composite developed of the 19 respondents who were mentored revealed that mentoring occurred at various stages of the participants' careers. Regardless of the time that mentoring first occurred, 79% of the participants stated that mentoring was important for career advancement and empowerment.

Core Themes: Research Question 1

Invariant themes within the analysis of the lived experience of each participant were identified based on the results of the study. Themes that emerged suggested that the role of a mentor in empowering African American healthcare professionals varies according to the needs of the mentee. The in-depth interview of each participant was mined to identify the core theme according to the two research questions. The core themes that were identified fell in two primary categories: the role of a mentor and the importance of mentoring in their own professional advancement.

Six core themes emerged from the analysis regarding the role of a mentor: (a) someone who helps bring out one's best which in turn assists in achieving goals, (b) someone who assists in problem solving, (c) someone who has professional experience in a relevant area, (d) someone with whom the mentee establishes a personal relationship,

(e) someone who is a good listener, and (f) someone who sets an example or serves as a role model. Further analysis of the data revealed a second category outlining the importance of mentoring in professional advancement.

Theme 1: A Mentor is Someone Who Helps Bring out One's Best

The first theme of what a mentor is describes a mentor as someone who can help the mentee to identify and exhibit his or her best qualities. Common comments among the participants described the mentor as someone who can assist the mentee to get to the next level of his or her career.

> That bridge if you will from the aspirers to the ones that have obtained where the aspirers want to be . . . that mentor in the middle. If I would have had from my early years a person that I respected, I wanted to be where he or she was and they gave me some opportunities to exhibit some quality . . . that would have meant the entire world to me. I wouldn't be here, I can tell you that, but my whole life would have been different. But as it was you're thrown to the world, you do the best you can, etc. It wasn't that bad but with a mentor it would have made a difference (Participant 1).

Having a mentor during the early years of the participant's career provides empowerment and may help with professional guidance for individuals who are inexperienced as to which career path to take (de Janasz, Sullivan, & Whiting, 2003; Thomas, 2001). But most important, a mentor can provide guidance to the mentee on how to achieve his or her career goals (Jenkins, 2005). Identifying strengths and areas for improvement early in one's career can help to prevent impending obstacles, therefore providing opportunities to fast tract that career.

Being able to identify with the organizational leaders also serves as a way to empower young professionals. Identifying with those who are in positions that these junior professionals aspire to be makes his or her goals appear to be more achievable. Furthermore, having the opportunity to interact with members of the leadership team provides an opportunity to network and display one's talents (Thomas, 2001).

> Just in working with my mentor I was able to see that people in upper management are real people, not just scary figures, they are real people. They have similar interests and you don't want to waste their time. When you meet with them it's not a time for BS, it's a time to talk about what's needed and then moving forward, so this has definitely helped me with my interactions (Participant 3).

Other study participants described their mentors as

> Someone in the organization that will take you and guide you and help you to learn your job so that you can be better at what you do. Someone who will help you along the way, who serves as a resource (Participant 4).

"My mentor was one who had the ability to force me to think about things and I didn't even know that he was actually having an impact upon me" (Participant 7). "Someone who helps you set goals and objectives, helps you get there in reaching those goals and objectives" (Participant 9).

The review of the literature in Chapter 2 discussed the benefits of mentoring on fast tracking a career. Caucasian professionals who are identified early in their careers as potential leaders and are mentored and interacted with organizational leaders often achieve career success in less time than African Americans who are usually recognized later in their careers (Thomas, 2001). Applying the same principle of identifying high performing African American professionals early in their careers could also be potentially beneficial for professional advancement (Larson, 2006; Thomas, 2001). The statements made by the participants (Participant 1, 3, 4, 7, & 9) lent credence to the fast that mentoring can be beneficial in helping young professionals perform at their best and learn the culture of the organization (Larson, 2006).

Theme 2: A Mentor Is a Problem Solver

A mentor is someone who can help the mentee with problem situations. It is not the mentor's primary responsibility to solve the problem per se, instead the role of the mentor is to turn the problem solving into problem management (Dancer, 2003). Learning by example is a key factor during a mentoring relationship. "To me a mentor is a teacher, someone with professional experience that you are trying to acquire that's willing to give of himself" (Participant 5). The mentee does not necessarily seek someone to pave the way, but instead seeks someone who can provide guidance, offer pearls of wisdom, and be available to give support when needed.

Similar to the role of teaching, effective mentoring means helping the person who is being mentored to be able to handle challenges, make the right decisions in stressful situations, and being able to effectively manage problems especially those involving upper level management. Daily challenges in the workplace can become discouraging to young professionals especially minorities who often feel as if they do not have the support of their Caucasian colleagues or come to believe that fellow employee cannot understand their frustration. African Americans junior professionals need to find comfort in knowing that they do have the support of someone who has experienced what they are currently experiencing and can empathize with them.

> If you are an African American in health care and if you are sincerely trying to advance, it's not easy trying to do it on your own. You have to have someone to support you and that is also recognized by others already as being a leader (Participant 12).

Having a mentor can help to reassure junior African American professionals that the challenges that they are encountering are a part of the process of professional advancement. The key to the success of young African American healthcare professionals is knowing how to resolve problems and being aware of the resources that are available to them (Dancer, 2003).

Theme 3: A Mentor is Someone who has Experience in the Relevant Area

The third theme of a mentor being someone who is experienced in the relevant area suggested that the participants found it beneficial to have mentors whose support extended beyond the personal level, and were instrumental in providing professional advice that was specific to the mentees' area of interest. Specialty areas within hospitals have different cultures, and although hospital organizations in general have a unique culture, there are also subcultures that exist within each specialty area within the organization. There is a need for mentors to take the mentee and provide individualized guidance. "Mentoring to me is taking someone under your wing and helping to guide them and grow professionally. The act of mentoring to me is a more willful deliberative act, it's not a passive" (Participant 7).

> To me it's a relationship that's established in a deliberate manner. You take someone under your wing. Or in your line, it doesn't matter what line, but you take them under your guidance and you're gonna provide them with leadership (Participant 8).

"Mentoring is to have someone in a leadership position that has experience in a particular area where you'd like to go or that you think that you would like to achieve" (Participant 12).

African American healthcare professionals have less opportunity of having the necessary exposure to the key decision makers within the organization. Networking with the key decision makers provides the opportunity for interactions with individuals within the organization who can play an influential role in career advancement (Dancer, 2003). Networking opportunities often occurs in places outside of the work environment. As previously stated African Americans are often excluded from these after hours social gatherings and therefore are usually a step behind their Caucasian counterparts with equal or less experience. For this reason it is important that his or her mentor is someone who not only has experience in the relevant area, but is also respected and socially connected within the organization.

Theme 4: A Mentor Is Someone with Whom You Can Establish a Personal Relationship

Participants expressed the importance and value of the relationship that they develop with their mentors and stressed that oftentimes the relationship starts as a friendship and later develops into a relationship where the senior colleagues identifies the junior professional's potential and a mentoring relationship is developed. In other situations where the relationship started out in a professional manner it slowly extended beyond the professional boundaries and a personal relationship was started. It is uncertain if this relationship occurs among other ethnic groups who are being mentored, however, one participant described the relationship with his mentor as "a big brother, a father, a teacher, a counselor, coach, all of the above" (Participant 8). Participant 7 stated that

> I felt that my mentor was like a father, he was like family and that gave me a very strong emotional feeling knowing that he was present and that he was always there for me. Those were the kinds of things that I think that over time you begin to realize that a great mentoring it really does become a very personal matter.

Theme 5: A Mentor Is a Good Listener

The mentee should know what his or her needs are. It is not the responsibility of the mentor to tell the mentee what to do. Instead, the mentee should have goals and objective so that the mentor can provide guidance (Kirk, 1991). In order to provide guidance, the mentor must be an active listener, because it may be possible that what the mentee is expressing and what his or her talents are do not align with that person's goals and objective.

Additionally, based on the fourth theme, the participants expressed that their definition of a mentor is someone who they feel comfortable with, someone who is like "a big brother, father, teacher, counselor" (Participant 7). This is an individual who listens with an attentive ear, someone who is available to not only provide advice, but just listen without saying anything, someone who is like a sounding board. The mentor as a listener compliments the personal nature of the relationship and helps to build camaraderie and trust in the relationship. A mentor is "someone who provides a listening ear and serves as a sounding board for my ideas my thoughts, any issues or problems I may be having and that person provides you with some guidance from their experience base" (Participant 22).

Effective mentoring requires a skilled mentor, one who possesses qualities that are valuable for professional advancement. Specifically these are qualities such as respect, empathy, integrity, and good listening skills. Mentors show motivation and enthusiasm that help to encourage and motivate the mentee (Dancer, 2003).

Theme 6: A Mentor Is a Role Model

The theme of a mentor being a role model is important not only to the person who is being mentored, but also instrumental in the leadership qualities that the current mentee will portray. The mentee emulates and sometimes aspires to be like the person that is providing mentoring. Climbing the corporate ladder is one key to success, however, professionalism and diplomacy, and overall professional etiquette is important in order to be respected.

In saying that, it is the mentor's responsibility to provide professional guidance that is both morally, ethically, and politically correct. "Mentoring for me was teaching professionalism and how to act accordingly; teaching diplomacy and tact" (Participant 11). However, in order for the mentor to be viewed as a role model for the mentee, both individuals must be able to see each other's strengths.

A close mentoring relationship with the mentor and mentee is needed. They must both be able to see some part of themselves in the other person. The protégé's desire to be like the mentor and the mentor identifying with the protégé as being similar to who he or she once was is needed to build a close relationship (Thomas, 2001). After a close relationship is established, a level of comfort develops where both individuals can see beyond the other's weaknesses (Thomas, 2001). Participant 16 described a mentor as "an experienced individual who can share insight and provide specific guidance on how to achieve goals and in the process how to avoid de-railers."

Core Theme: Research Question Two

Theme One: Mentoring is Important for Professional Advancement

The second category revealed a common theme regarding the value of mentorship in professional advancement. The theme in this category was generated from responses pertaining to the second research question. The key theme regarding the importance of mentoring in professional advancement was that mentoring is very important for African Americans hospital professionals to advance to the decision-making positions in their careers. Seventy nine percent the participants stated that mentoring was important, with 57.9% reporting that it is very important for career advancement.

Participants believed that a mentor helped them to deal with frustrations, "we need to know that the plight that we're having, or the concerns or the frustrations are just natural for who we are and where we are going" (Participant 20). Mentors provide their mentees with information about the daily operations of organization that otherwise they would not have known. Other reasons why mentoring was considered to be important is to provide guidance and support for African Americans who have the desire to advance in their careers and require an experience individual to help guide them in making career decisions. It is believed that a mentor can provide the insight on organizational operation, especially skills that are learned through experience.

Often it is the unspoken cultural criteria that help to fast tract one's career. Some African Americans may not have the family background that places them in the right situation for networking or the right exposure that will give them the needed preparation (Jenkins, 2005). One participant reported,

> There definitely are some inherent things in the system that are not necessarily to our advantage, that we are not taught, per se, but are things that you find out the hard way, so I think having a mentor absolutely was helpful (Participant 14).

The importance of mentoring as a key theme in professional advancement aligns with the core themes is the first category. Mentors can be the conduit for the mentee to gain access in social and professional "circles" that may not be accessible to minorities such as African Americans.

A mentor helps the mentee to build a large diverse network of long-term relationships. This network of individuals should be a heterogeneous group so that the mentee can gain the pearls necessary to fast tract his or her career. Sometimes members of this group may play specific roles that serve as the building blocks for success.

In addition to having a network of African Americans who can provide valuable social support, the mentee should also have individuals from other ethnic groups to (a) provide him or her with exposure to other cultures, as this is important in becoming an organizational leader; and (b) provide access and exposure to the key decision makers in the organization, especially in situations where there is limited diversity among individuals at the highest level of the organization.

It has been reported that mentoring is important in empowering junior professionals. Professional achievements have been directly correlated to the guidance of a mentor. The literature shows that individuals who have been mentored receive higher compensation, advance more quickly, and express greater satisfaction as compared to those who were not (de Janasz et al., 2003). As stated by one of the participants, "I think you're much more likely to achieve your goals of growing in an organization with the help of a mentor" (Participant 16).

An unpredicted finding in this study revealed that the racial and gender demographics of the mentor was not important. Fifty two percent ($n = 11$) of the study participants had a mentor of different ethnicity, and 33% ($n = 7$) had a mentor of a different gender. Although this finding was unexpected, it might be a result of the need for diversity and promotion of African Americans to upper level positions. Fifty seven percent ($n = 12$) of the participants chose their mentors, however, it is uncertain if they would have chosen an African American mentor if the choice was available.

There continues to be limited number of chief operating officer, chief executive officer, director of nursing, and vice president of nursing to name a few (Griffin, 2001; Woog, 2005). However, as awareness of diversity in healthcare, especially in hospitals, increases, the possibility of having African American role models at the highest level of the hospital organization also increases. The increase in African American hospital decision makers may empower young African American junior hospital professional to fast tract their careers. Unlike their Caucasian colleagues, African Americans in healthcare progress slowly at the beginning of their careers and are not recognized as high performers until later after becoming midlevel managers (Thomas, 2001). The slow career start often leads to discouragement and lack of motivation, resulting in poor representation at the top level of the organization (Voges, 2006).

Limitations

Limitations of this study are provided to identify potential weaknesses of the current study. This qualitative case study was limited by several factors. The honesty of each participant response during the interview, the validity of the interview questions that were used, and the number of African Americans working in healthcare in a decision-making capacity in the southeastern United States are limitations.

The purpose of a qualitative study is to explore a phenomenon and to identify common themes among individuals in the study. The total number of participants who consented to participate in this study was 21 although the research investigator's initial intent was to include a sample of 30. The number of participants of the study was limited to 21 because of the number of African American hospital decision makers in the geographical area who consented to participate in the study. The reason for the reduced number of participants was primarily due to the limited number of participants meeting the inclusion criteria of (a) a decision maker in a hospital or inpatient care facility that is affiliated with a hospital that has at least 300 inpatient beds; (b) a hospital decision maker that is employed in the specialty area of nursing, medicine, administration, and pharmacy whose position is at a director level or above; and (c) a hospital decision maker who would consent to participate in the study by participating in a live interview.

Fifty nine potential participants were contacted to participate by using a referral snowball method of sampling. The individuals were provided with an overview of the study and the purpose of the study. Each individual was also informed that his or her participation in the study was confidential, and that all unique identifier pertaining to the personal identification and place of employment would be excluded from the study analysis.

After three follow up letters or e-mails to request participation, 22 individuals consented to participate in the study. Each individual was assigned a number to enforce anonymity. After completing the informed consent, Participant Number 18 was unavailable due to time constraints. Therefore, the final participants who participated in the study are Participants 1-17 and 19-22.

Qualitative research with a large sample size may become problematic. Therefore, to prevent potential problems, phenomenological studies require 10 to 50 participants (Creswell, 2004). The sample size that was used for this qualitative study was 21, which is within the recommended range for a qualitative research.

The second limitation was due to time restraints of the participants. Twenty of the 21 participants who participated in the study were employed in Florida. The two major reasons why individuals did not participate in the study were time constraints and non response. The geographical demographics of these study participants have influenced the outcome because of the diversity or lack of diversity in the hospitals that are located in this area.

The strengths of the study included the diverse group of individuals who consented to participate. These individuals included hospital CEO, directors, males, and females. Four specialty areas were represented: medicine, nursing, pharmacy, and administration. This diverse group of hospital professionals provided a subjective view of the lived experiences of mentoring and professional advancement for African Americans.

The second strength of the study was the sample size and method of data collection. Interviewing 21 individuals to explore their lived experiences as it pertains to mentoring and professional advancement provided extensive subjective information from the participants. The detailed interviews were captured via tape recording that provided accuracy to ensure that the themes that were identified were accurate according to the participants' recall of events that occurred during their professional career.

Significance of the Study

The significance of this study was to determine the role of mentoring in professional advancement and to determine if mentoring is important in career advancement of African Americans healthcare professionals working in a hospital setting. The data from the 21 participants were mined and common themes were identified to answer the two research questions. The invariant themes that emerged from the study suggested that mentoring is important in the professional advancement of African Americans who are on the professional path for career advancement. Additional themes also suggested that the role of a mentor is not specific to one description but varies according to the needs of the mentee. The six key themes that identified the role of a mentor are someone who (a) helps bring out one's best which in turn assists in achieving goals, (b) a problem solver, (c) an experienced individual in the area of the mentee's specialty, (d) is personable, (e) is a good listener, and (f) is a role model.

Significance of the Study to Leadership

The knowledge that was acquired from this study helps to support findings in the literature that was not specific to the sample that was included in this study. The findings based on this current sample of individuals suggest that African Americans who were mentored and were decision makers at the time of the study believed that having a mentor helped them to navigate their career by providing both personal and professional guidance and support. This study showed that leadership using the Path Goal Model of leadership may be instrumental in empowering African Americans through mentoring.

According to the Path Goal Model leadership theory, leaders can have an impact on their subordinates by providing motivation which influences their performance, and increases the overall satisfaction of their job. By using this leadership model, African American healthcare professionals can work collaboratively with their mentors to develop goals and outline a path that will fast tract their careers (Longest et al., 2000). In addition, the results of this study revealed that mentoring is a characteristic of leadership that can be applied to provide role modeling and support for minorities and other individuals who may not have the networking capabilities or the expertise to avoid career obstacle (Thomas, 2001).

This study also revealed that mentoring is a form of leadership in that it helps to empower those who under different circumstances may not advance as quickly as they would with a mentor. The leader who serves as mentors for junior hospital professionals provides a work environment that supports the development of future leaders of the organizations. Mentees often emulate their mentors; therefore, both mentor and mentees have the advantage of learning from each other and thereby growing professionally.

Recommendations

Recommendations can be made to hospital leaders and researchers. The first recommendation is for hospital leaders to implement a formal mentoring program within their organization. This program would include the availability of mentors for individuals within the organization who are on a career path to a decision-making position.

Hospital organizations do not have the level of diversity that is needed to accurately represent the population that they serve. This study showed that a mentoring is an important tool to help fast tract the careers of African Americans, thereby increasing diversity within the organization. A structured mentoring program will also help to alleviate some of the potential obstacles that young professional encounter. It can help to provide emotional support as reported by some of the participants in this study in that they will be able to identify with someone who has traveled the path that they are currently traveling.

The second recommendation to hospital leaders is to develop a mentoring program where members of the leadership team can interact with lower level individuals who have a desire to better understand the daily operations of the organization. This interaction with hospital leaders should complement the mentees' interaction with his or her mentor. This program should include an open-door policy where junior level professionals can discuss the various opportunities that are available to them.

This will assist them in identifying their professional needs so that they can determine what characteristics they should identify when choosing their ideal mentor. This will help them to set realistic expectations and outline goals and objectives that will assist them in reaching their expected level of achievement. The focus of the mentoring program should not be specific to same race or same gender mentoring relationships. Instead, heterogeneous mentoring relationships should be encouraged and in some situations the mentee may require multiple mentors to provide exposures to his or her diverse professional needs.

Recommendations for Future Study

There are several recommendations that can be made for future studies based on the results of this study. First recommendation is to repeat the study in a larger geographical region. The results should be compared to determine if the findings can be applied to a national sample. The participants in this study were limited to a specific region, therefore as a result of the outcome of this study it is necessary to determine if the results are applicable to a similar group in a nationwide study.

Based on the results of this study which evaluated the lived experiences of African-Americans, it would also be beneficial to conduct a similar study to evaluate the perception of mentoring among hospital professionals from various ethnic groups. The purpose of this study is to better understand if there are similarities regarding the perceived benefits of mentoring among other ethnicities. This study would gather data on the cultural experiences of mentoring and provide a better understanding of mentoring and empowerment across various ethnic groups.

An additional recommendation is to conduct a longitudinal study evaluating African American and Caucasian hospital decision makers and the impact of mentoring on the timeline of their professional advancement. This study should be conducted using a quantitative methodology with a sample size of at least 200. The recommended study duration should be at least five years in order to accurately capture the rate of professional advancement. The potential benefit of this study is to add to the body of literature by (a) providing data on the rate of professional advancement for African

Americans as compared to Caucasian who are mentored, (b) provide information regarding the participants perception of the benefit is any of a mentor, (c) and evaluate the differences if any of the role of the mentor in each group.

The final recommendation for additional studies is to conduct a study comparing professional advancement of African Americans who were mentored early in their careers to those who were not mentored. This study would help to determine the number of years it takes for both groups to achieve the same level of professional advancement. This study would also provide more evidence regarding the impact that mentoring has on professional advancement.

Conclusions

This study of 21 African American hospital decision makers adds to the body of literature confirming that mentoring plays a significant role in the career advancement of junior professionals. This study was conducted to explore the lived experiences of African American decision makers employed in a hospital setting as it pertains to mentoring and professional advancement. The analysis of the data revealed that a mentor provides both professional and emotional support for young African Americans who aspire to become organizational leaders. Additionally, the participants of this study reported that not only did their mentors help them in advancing to their current position, but mentoring was an important factor for their professional advancement. The study adds to the body of literature that supports mentoring in other disciplines, and it is recommended that the results of this study be used to encourage organizational leaders to support both tenured and novice African American hospital professionals by implementing a formal mentoring program within their organization to support those who aspire to advance up the cooperate ladder.

REFERENCES

A race ethnicity comparison of career attainments in healthcare management. (2002). Retrieved June 6, 2005 from http://www.ache.org/PUBS/Research/RaceEthnic ExecutiveSummary2002.pdf

Affinity Groups. (2004). Retrieved June 6, 2005 from http://www.lilly.com/careers/ diversity/affinity_groups/index.html

Ambrose, L. (2003). Mentoring diversity: Serving a diverse patient population calls for diverse leadership. *American College of Healthcare Executives*. Retrieved June 28, 2005 from http://www.ache.org/newclub/CAREER/MentorArticles/ Diversity.cfm

Anonymous. (2004/2005, Winter). A healthy increase in the number of blacks in academic nursing. *Journal of Blacks in Higher Education, 46,* 40-44. Retrieved January 17, 2007 from ProQuest database.

Barrett, I., Cervero, R., & Johnson-Bailey, J. (2004). The career development of black human resources developers in the United States. *Human Resource Development International, 7*(1), 5-100. Retrieved November 2, 2006 from EBSCOhost database.

Bernstein, L. (2007). Is there a mentor in your future? *Career World*, *35*(4), 9-11. Retrieved January 14, 2007 from EBSCOhost database.

Bilchik, G. S. (May, 2000). The slow road to executive diversity. *Hospitals & Health Networks, 74*(5), 34-39. Retrieved March 19, 2005 from EBSCOhost database.

Blancero, D. M., & DelCampo, R. G. (2005). Hispanics in the workplace: Experiences with mentoring and networking. *Employment Relations Today (Wiley), 32*(2), 31-38. Retrieved November 4, 2006 from EBSCOhost database.

Bohne, P. (2003). Breaking through the ceiling. *Marketing Health Services, 23*(3), 14-20. Retrieved January 14, 2007 from EBSCOhost database.

Brush, B., Sochaiski, J., & Berger, A. (2004). Imported care: Recruiting foreign nurses to U.S. healthcare facilities. *Health Affairs, 23*(3), 78-88. Retrieved June 19, 2005 from EBSCOhost database.

Bureau of Labor Statistics. (n.d.). *Pharmacists*. Retrieved June 6, 2005 from http://stats.bls.gov/oco/pdf/ocos079.pdf

Bureau of Labor Statistics. (2004). *Household data annual averages*. Retrieved June 6, 2005 from http://bls.gov/cps/cpsaat11.pdf

Choudhuri, D., Glauser, A., & Peregoy, J. (2004). Guidelines for writing a qualitative manuscript for the Journal of Counseling & Development. *Journal of Counseling & Development*, *82,* 43-46. Retrieved January 14, 2007 from EBSCOhost database.

Cooper, D. R., & Schindler, P. S. (2002). *Business research methods* (8th ed.). Boston: Irwin.

Creswell, J. W. (2003). *Research Design: Qualitative, Quantitative, and Mixed Methods of Approaches* (2nd ed.). Upper Saddle River, NJ: Merrill Prentice Hall.

Creswell, J. W. (2004). *Educational research: Planning, conducting, and evaluating quantitative and qualitative research* (2nd ed.). Upper Saddle River, NJ: Merrill Prentice Hall.

Dancer, J. M. (2003). Mentoring in healthcare: Theory in search of practice? *Clinician in Management, 12*, 21-31. Retrieved May 30, 2005 from EBSCOhost database.

De Janasz, S., Sullivan, S., & Whiting, V. (November, 2003). Mentors network and career success: Lessons for turbulent times. *Academy of Management Executive, 17*(4), 78-91. Retrieved May 26, 2007 from EBSCOhost database.

Dolan, T. C. (2004, September/October). Mentoring at every level. *Healthcare Executive,* 6-7. Retrieved May 30, 2005 from EBSCOhost database.

Edmondson Bell, E., & Nkomo, S. (2003). Our separate ways: Black and White women and the struggle for professional identity. *The Diversity Factor*, *11*(1), 11-16. Retrieved May 30, 2005 from EBSCOhost database.

Encarta Dictionary Tools. (2006). Retrieved May 12, 2005 from http://encarta.msn. com/encnet/features/dictionary/dictionaryhome.aspx

Evans, M. (2004, September). Healthcare's minority report. *Modern Healthcare, 34*(39), 6-7, 14. Retrieved May 13, 2005 from ProQuest database.

Fagenson, E. & Amendola, K. (1993). TQM--Total quality mentoring. Factors influencing mentoring functions provided and received. *Academy of Management Proceeding.* 58-62. Retrieved October 2005 from EBSCOhost database.

Fewer foreign docs. (2004). *Modern Healthcare, 34*(12), 25. Retrieved January 14, 2007 from EBSCOhost database.

Fracaro, K. (2006). Mentoring for career guidance. *Supervision, 67*(6), 13-16. Retrieved January 14, 2007 from EBSCOhost database.

Gartland, J. J., Hojat, M., Christian, E. B., Callahan, C. A., & Nasca, T. J. (2003). African American and White physicians: A comparison of satisfaction with medical education, professional careers, and research activities. *Teaching & Learning in Medicine, 15*(2), 106-112. Retrieved January 18, 2007 from EBSCOhost database.

Gathers, D. (2003). Diversity management: An imperative for healthcare organizations. *Hospital Topics, 81*(3), 14-20. Retrieved May 6, 2005 from EBSCOhost database.

Gonzalez-Figueroa, E., & Young, A. (2005). Ethnic identity and mentoring among Latinas in professional roles. *Cultural Diversity & Ethnic Minority Psychology, 11*(3), 213-226. Retrieved January 14, 2007 from EBSCOhost database.

Gonzalez-Figueroa, E., & Young, N. (2006). Diversity in the executive suite. *Modern Healthcare, 36*(5), 6-30. Retrieved October 1, 2006 from EBSCOhost database.

Griffin, M. (2001). The healthcare industry: Multi-disciplinary opportunities leading to careers in healthcare. *The Black Collegian Online.* Retrieved December 27, 2005 from http://www.black-collegian.com/issues/2005-05/health.shtml

Gwyther, M. (2006). What they want is autonomy. *Management Today, 5*. Retrieved December 12, 2006 from EBSCOhost database.

Heckathorn, D. D. (2002). Respondent-driven sampling II: Deriving valid population estimates from chain-referral samples of hidden populations. *Social Problems, 49*(1), 11-34. Retrieved March 28, 2007 from http://www.columbia.edu/~mjs2105/heckathorn02.pdf

Heggins, W. (2004). Preparing African American males for the professoriate: Issues and challenges. *Western Journal of Black Studies, 28*(2), 354-365. Retrieved January 17, 2007 from EBSCOhost database.

Hellinghausen, M. A. (2000). Closing the gap: Program aims to add more minorities to healthcare professions. *Healthy People 2010.* Retrieved June 12, 2006 from EBSCOhost database.

Institute for Diversity in Health Management. (2006, July 23). *Hospitalconnect.com.* Retrieved August 1, 2007 from http://www.diversityconnection.org/diversityconnection_app/news-and-events/News_index.jsp?fll=S8&sll=S80

Interviews and the philosophy of qualitative research. (2004). *Journal of Higher Education, 75*(1), 127-132. Retrieved January 14, 2007 from EBSCOhost database.

Ivey, M. F. (2005). Rationale for having a chief pharmacy officer in a health care organization. *American Journal of Health-System Pharmacy, 62*(9), 975-979. Retrieved June 5, 2005 from EBSCOhost database.

Jandeska, K., & Kraimer, M. (2005). Women's perception of organizational culture, work attitudes, and role-modeling behaviors. *Journal of Managerial Issues, 17*(4), 461-478. Retrieved January 14, 2007 from EBSCOhost database.

Jenkins, M. (2005). Why you need a mentor. *Black Enterprise, 35*(8), 80-86. Retrieved July 14, 2007 from EBSCOhost database.

Kelly, J. (2006). Diversity programs help midlevel managers climb the executive ladder. *AHA News, 42*(24), 6. Retrieved December 14, 2006 from EBSCOhost database.

Kirk, J. (1991). Life cycle of a mentoring relationship. *University Mentoring Manual*, Western Carolina University, WRIGHT. Retrieved November 19, 2006 from Florida State University Library.

Kogler Hill, K. & Gant, G. (Spring/Summer 2000). Mentoring by minorities for minorities: The organizational communication support program. *Review of Business, 21*(1/2), 53-58. Retrieved October, 2006 from EBSCOhost database.

Koopman, R. J., & Thiedke, C. C. (2005). Views of family medicine department chairs about mentoring junior faculty. *Medical Teacher, 27*(8), 734-737. Retrieved December 27, 2006 from EBSCOhost database.

Kram, K. E. (1985). *Mentoring at work.* Lanham, MD: University Press of America. Retrieved June 5, 2005 from EBSCOhost database.

Larson, L. (2006). Getting to the 'C Suite.' *Trustee, 59*(3), 12-19. Retrieved December 27, 2006 from EBSCOhost database.

Late, M. (2004). Actions urged to increase numbers of U.S. minority health workers. *Nation's Health, 34*(9), 1-14. Retrieved January 14, 2007 from EBSCOhost database.

Leadership development program for recent graduates, helping recent graduates rise to the top. (n.d.). Retrieved May 14, 2005 from http://www.jnj.com/careers/leaderprog.html

Leedy, P. D., & Ormrod, J. E. (2001). *Practical research: Planning and design* (7th ed.). Upper Saddle River, NJ: Merrill Prentice Hall.

Lockwood, N. R. (2005). Workplace diversity: Leveraging the power of difference for competitive advantage. *HR Magazine, 50*(6), 1-10. Retrieved October 2, 2005 from EBSCOhost database.

Longest, B., Rakich, J., & Darr, K. (2000). *Managing Health Services Organizations and Systems* (4th ed.). Baltimore, MD: Health Profession Press.

Maslow, A. H. (1943). A theory of human motivation. *Psychological Review, 50*, 133-158. Retrieved November 19, 2006 from Florida State University Library.

May, E. L. (2003). Mentoring: Why it should be your personal and professional priority. *Healthcare Executive, 18*(6), 6-13. Retrieved May 29, 2005 from EBSCOhost database.

McCluskey, N. (2005). Embrace mentoring. *Massage Magazine,* (113), 20-22. Retrieved January 14, 2007 from EBSCOhost database.

McGlowan-Fellows, B., & Thomas, C. (2005). Changing roles: Corporate mentoring of black women. *International Journal of Mental Health, 33*(4), 3-18. Retrieved October 25, 2006 from EBSCOhost database.

Meltzoff, J. (2003). *Critical Thinking about Research.* Washington, DC: American Psychological Association.

Merriam-Webster Online Dictionary. (2007). Retrieved March 28, 2007 from http://www.m-w.com/

Moustakas, C. (1994). *Phenomenological Research Methods.* Thousand Oaks, CA: Sage Publications.

Neil, R. (2003, December). Getting ahead. Diversity becoming a part of hospitals business practice. *Materials Management in Healthcare,* 14-17. Retrieved May 13, 2005 from ProQuest database.

Nold, E., & Sander, W. (2004). Role of the director of pharmacy: The first six months. *American Journal of Health-System Pharmacy, 61*, 2294-2310. Retrieved June 6, 2005 from EBSCOhost database.

North, A., Johnson, J., Knotts, K., & Whelan, L. (2006). Ground instability with mentoring. *Nursing Management, 37*(2), 16-18. Retrieved January 14, 2007 from EBSCOhost database.

Pappas, J. M., Flaherty, K. E., &Wooldridge, B. (2003). Achieving strategic consensus in the hospital setting: A middle management perspective. *Hospital Topics, 81*(1), 15-22. Retrieved June 12, 2005 from EBSCOhost database.

Patton, M. W. (2002). *Qualitative Research & Evaluation Methods* (3rd ed.). Thousand Oaks, Ca: Sage Publications.

Pieper, S. (2004). The mentoring cycle: A six-phase process for success. *Healthcare Executive, 19*(6), 16-18. Retrieved January 14, 2007 from EBSCOhost database.

Ragin, B. R. (1997). Diversified mentoring relationships in organizations: A power perspective. *Academy of Management Review, 22*(2), 482-522. Retrieved October 21, 2005 from EBSCOhost database.

Rajan, A., & Harris, S. (2003, September 9). What works, what doesn't, and why. *Personnel Today,* 19-20. Retrieved April 27, 2005 from EBSCOhost database.

Ralston, P. (2003). Diversifying the health professions: A model program. *American Journal of Behavior, 27*(3), 235-245. Retrieved June 12, 2005 from EBSCOhost database.

Reilly, P. (2003). Minority report. *Modern Healthcare, 33*(32), 14. Retrieved June 12, 2005 from ProQuest database.

Romano, M. (2004). Minority hires still lagging. *Modern Healthcare, 34*(24), 24-28. Retrieved January 14, 2007 from EBSCOhost database.

Russell, C. K., & Gregory, D. M. (2003). Evaluation of qualitative research studies. *Evidence Based Nursing, 6,* 36-40. Retrieved February 14, 2007 from EBSCOhost database.

Salkind, A. (2003). *Exploring research* (5th ed.). Upper Saddle River, NJ: Prentice Hall, Inc.

Sanders, L., & Bowcutt, M. (2004, September/October). CEO/CNO relationship survey findings. *Healthcare Executive*. Retrieved January 13, 2007 from http://www.ache.org/PUBS/Research/pdf/CEO_CNO_Survey.PDF

Sanders, M. & Sillers, T. (2000). I hope you dance (Recorded by Lee Ann Womack). On *I hope you dance* (CD). Nashville, Tennessee: Mercury Records.

Scott, M. (2006). Minority Report. *Hospital & Health Networks, 80*(9), 16-18. Retrieved December 14, 2006 from EBSCOhost database.

Shaffer, B., Tallarica, B., & Walsh, J. (2000). Start mentoring today for satisfaction, inspiration, and nurse retention. *Nursing Management, 31*(1), 32-34. Retrieved May 30, 2005 from EBSCOhost database.

Strategies for leadership: Does your hospital reflect the community it serves? (n.d.). *ache.org*. Retrieved June 6, 2005 from http://www.hospitalconnect.com/aha/key_issues/disparity/content/DiversityTool.pdf

Stokes, P. (2003). Exploring the relationship between mentoring and counseling. *British Journal of Guidance & Counseling, 31*(1), 25-40. Retrieved June 12, 2006 from EBSCOhost database.

Supporting our diverse culture: Exploring diverse interest and cultural heritage. (n.d.). Electronically retrieved March 27, 2004 from http://www.jnj.com/careers/support.html

Shur Bilchik, G. The show road to executive diversity. *Hospitals and Health Networks, 74*(5), 34-39. Retrieved June 27, 2006 from ProQuest database.

Szabo, J. (2004). U.S. healthcare spending hits record $1.6 trillion. *Physicians Financial News, 22*(3), 17. Retrieved June 5, 2005 from ProQuest database.

The Black Perspective Online. (2000). Supporting minorities in healthcare. Electronically retrieved March 27, 2004 from http://www.blackperspective.com/pages/minorities_healthcare.html

Thomas, D. (2001). The truth about mentoring minorities: Race matters. *Harvard Business Review, 79*(4), 98-107. Retrieved October 12, 2005 from EBSCOhost database.

Tourigny, L., & Pulich, M. (2005). A critical examination and informal mentoring among nurses. *The Healthcare Manager, 24*(1), 68-76. Retrieved May 30, 2005 from EBSCOhost database.

U.S. Department of Labor: Bureau of Labor Statistics. (2006). Retrieved September 20, 2006 from http://www.bls.gov/oes/current/naics4_622100.htm#b11-0000

Voges, N. (2006). Diversity in the executive suite. *Modern Healthcare, 36*(15), 6-30. Retrieved January 5, 2007 from EBSCOhost database.

Washington, D., Erickson, J. I., & Ditomassi, M. (2004). Mentoring the minority nurse leaders of tomorrow. *Nurse Administration Quarterly, 28*(3), 165-169. Retrieved March 24, 2005 from EBSCOhost database.

Weil, P. A. (2003). A race/ethnic comparison of career attainments in healthcare management. *Healthcare Executive, 18*(6), 22-26. Retrieved May 6, 2005 from EBSCOhost database.

Woog, D. (2005). *Diversity in Healthcare*. Retrieved May 16, 2005 from http://www.featuredreports.monster.com/diversityhc/overview/

Worth, P. (2004, April). The evolution of diversity in nursing and nurse anesthesia. *American Association of Nurse Anesthetists Journal, 72*(2), 101-105. Retrieved May 31, 2005 from EBSCOhost database.

Yin, R. K. (1994). *Case study research: Designs and methods* (2nd ed.). Thousand Oaks, CA: Sage Publications Inc.

Zachary, B., Gilbert, L., & Gragg, M. (1995). Director of nursing finance: Controlling healthcare cost. *Nursing Management, 26*(11), 49-53. Retrieved June 5, 2005 from EBSCOhost database.

APPENDIX A: INTRODUCTORY LETTER

APPENDIX A: INTRODUCTORY LETTER

Dear Healthcare Provider,

I am a student at the University of Phoenix working on a Doctorate Degree in Health Administration. I am conducting a research study entitled:
African American Decision Makers in Healthcare: Exploring the Impact of Mentoring on Professional Advancement.

The purpose of the research study is to evaluate the relationship between African Americans working in a hospital setting or inpatient care setting and the impact of mentoring on their professional advancement to decision-making positions.

I am contacting you to request your participation in this research study. The population that will be included in this research are African American healthcare professionals who are currently employed or have worked in the following areas during the past 12 months: administration, medicine, nursing, or pharmacy, and have decision-making responsibilities for the daily operation of a department and/or the hospital organization. The phenomenon being explored in this research is the impact of mentoring and empowerment among African American healthcare professionals.

Study participants should be employed at a director's level or above, or are influential in the daily operation of a department or the organization. Data collection for this research will consist of a short interview. Completion of the interview should take approximately 20-30 minutes. More detailed information and an informed consent will be given after you have expressed an interest in participating in the study.

If you have any questions I can be reached at 954-895-2033.

Deon Wolliston

University of Phoenix

School of Advance Studies

APPENDIX B: INFORMED CONSENT

APPENDIX B: INFORMED CONSENT

Dear Participant,

I am a student at the University of Phoenix working on a Doctorate Degree in Health Administration. I am conducting a research study entitled: *African American Decision Makers in Healthcare: Exploring the Impact of Mentoring on Professional Advancement.*

The purpose of this qualitative case study is to explore the lived experiences of African Americans in the healthcare industry as they pertain to mentoring opportunities and their professed impact on empowerment and advancement in their career.

Your participation will involve a live interview which will require your recall of events that occurred during your career in healthcare. Upon completion of data collection a follow up will be conducted after the interview is completed to verify that your responses to the questions have been interpreted accurately. Participation in this study is voluntary. If you choose not to participate or to withdraw from the study at any time, you may do so without penalty. The results of the research study may be published but your name will not be used and your information will be maintained in confidence. Information obtained as a result of your participation in this study will not include any unique identifier that will disclose the identity or place of employment of the research participant.

In this research, there are no foreseeable risks to study participants. The study will be conducted through a recorded interview process. The interview will consist of opened-ended questions. The total process is expected to last approximately 20-30 minutes. Your response to the interview questions will be recorded for accuracy.

Although there may be no direct benefit to you, your participation in this study will help to describe the possible benefits of mentoring in career advancement of African American healthcare professionals. Prior to your participation in the study, you will be given the opportunity to ask any questions that you may have regarding your participation in the study. An informed consent must be obtained prior to the commencement of the interview: therefore, your signature at the end of this document will serve as your consent to participate in the study. After signing the informed consent, please return it with an original signature within three business days to the address listed below.

If you have any questions concerning the research study, please contact me at 954-895-2033. Thank you for your participation and cooperation.

Sincerely,

Deon Wolliston

University of Phoenix

School of Advance Studies

By signing this form I acknowledge that I understand the nature of the study, the potential risks to me as a participant, and the means by which my identity will be kept confidential. My signature on this form also indicates that I am 18 years or older and that I give my permission to voluntarily serve as a participant in the study described.

____

Participant's Name Date

____

Participant's Signature Date

Return Address:

Deon Wolliston
17903 SW 35 Ct
Miramar, Florida
33029

APPENDIX C: CONFIDENTIALITY AGREEMENT

Confidentiality Agreement

To Whom It May Concern:

I am a student at the University of Phoenix completing a Doctorate degree in Health Administration. I am conducting a study entitled: *African American Decision Makers in Healthcare: Exploring the Impact of Mentoring on Professional Advancement.* Collection of data for this study will include a recorded interview that will outline lived experiences of the study participants. Access to this information is restricted to the research investigator, and members of the research committee. Due to the nature of the study other individuals will be contracted to transcribe and analyze data collected during the recorded interview. Each third party contractor is required to sign a confidentiality agreement.

The purpose of the confidentiality agreement is to ensure that there is an agreement between the researcher and all third party contractors that all information pertaining to the above named research will be kept confidential. Any information that is given during the interview will not be shared with anyone except the researcher and committee members. All written documents and tape recordings will be returned to the researcher within seven days after the contracted services have been completed. Additionally, any information pertaining to the research or information from the interview will not be duplicated. Return of all study materials, interviews (written or recorded) will be sent via secure mail which will include Federal Express, UPS, DHL, or Priority Mail to the address listed below. A return receipt and signature of receipt will be requested. Your signature at the end of this document will serve as an acceptance to all terms outlined above and the highest priority will be given to keeping all information pertaining to this study and the study participants confidential. Please sign and return this agreement to the address listed below.

By signing this form I acknowledge that I understand the nature of the study and steps to be utilized for keeping all information pertaining to this study confidential. I have accepted the terms outlined in this document and will handle all documents pertaining to this study with the highest level of confidentiality.

____

Name of Contractor/Company

____

Signature of Authorized Individual   Date

Return address: Deon Wolliston
17903 SW 35 Ct
Miramar, Fl
33029

Letter of Confidentiality

To Whom It May Concern:

I am a student at the University of Phoenix completing a Doctorate degree in Health Administration. I am conducting a study entitled: *African-American Decision Makers in Healthcare: Exploring the Impact of Mentoring on Professional Advancement.*

Collection of data for this study will include a recorded interview that will outline lived experiences of the study participants. Access to this information is restricted to the research investigator, and members of the research committee. Due to the nature of the study other individuals will be contracted to transcribe and analyze data collected during the recorded interview. Each third party contractor is required to sign a confidentiality agreement.

The purpose of the confidentiality agreement is to ensure that there is an agreement between the researcher and all third party contractors that all information pertaining to the above named research will be kept confidential. Any information that is given during the interview will not be shared with anyone except the researcher. All written document and tape recording will be returned to the researcher within seven days after the contracted services have been completed. Additionally, any information pertaining to the research or information from the interview will not be duplicated. Return of all study material, interview (written or recorded) will be send via secure mail which will include Federal Express, UPS, DHL, or Priority Mail to the address listed below. A return receipt and signature of receipt will be requested. Your signature at the end of this document will serve as an acceptance to all terms outlined above and the highest priority will be given to keeping all information pertaining to this study and the study participants confidential. Please sign and return this agreement to the address listed below.

By signing this form I acknowledge that I understand the nature of the study, the importance of keeping all information pertaining to this study confidential. I have accepted the terms outlined in this document and will handle all documents pertaining to this study with the highest level of confidentiality.

Marti B. Giroud

Name of Contractor/Company

MBGiroud 5/15/07

Signature of Authorized Individual Date

Return address:
Deon Wolliston
17903 SW 35 Ct
Miramar, Fl
33029

Letter of Confidentiality

To Whom It May Concern:

I am a student at the University of Phoenix completing a Doctorate degree in Health Administration. I am conducting a study entitled: *African-American Decision Makers in Healthcare: Exploring the Impact of Mentoring on Professional Advancement.*

Collection of data for this study will include a recorded interview that will outline lived experiences of the study participants. Access to this information is restricted to the research investigator, and members of the research committee. Due to the nature of the study other individuals will be contracted to transcribe and analyze data collected during the recorded interview. Each third party contractor is required to sign a confidentiality agreement.

The purpose of the confidentiality agreement is to ensure that there is an agreement between the researcher and all third party contractors that all information pertaining to the above named research will be kept confidential. Any information that is given during the interview will not be shared with anyone except the researcher. All written document and tape recording will be returned to the researcher within seven days after the contracted services have been completed. Additionally, any information pertaining to the research or information from the interview will not be duplicated. Return of all study material, interview (written or recorded) will be send via secure mail which will include Federal Express, UPS, DHL, or Priority Mail to the address listed below. A return receipt and signature of receipt will be requested. Your signature at the end of this document will serve as an acceptance to all terms outlined above and the highest priority will be given to keeping all information pertaining to this study and the study participants confidential. Please sign and return this agreement to the address listed below.

By signing this form I acknowledge that I understand the nature of the study, the importance of keeping all information pertaining to this study confidential. I have accepted the terms outlined in this document and will handle all documents pertaining to this study with the highest level of confidentiality.

John C. Caruso

Name of Contractor/Company

John C. Caruso 5-31-07

Signature of Authorized Individual Date

Return address:
Deon Wolliston
17903 SW 35 Ct
Miramar, Fl
33029

APPENDIX D: STUDY INTERVIEW QUESTIONS

Participant Number

Age

Position

Professional Degree

Number of Beds in the Organization

Size of Department and Number of Direct Reports if any?

1. How long have you been employed in healthcare? How long have you worked for your current organization?
2. Are you satisfied with your current job?
3. Do you feel that you have achieved your career goals?
4. What is the highest level of management in the organization that you believe that you will achieve?
5. Please explain why?
6. Were you mentored at any time during your career?
7. Please give your definition of mentoring.
8. Describe the role of your mentor.
9. At what point in your career did you have your first interaction with a mentor?
10. For what period during your professional career in a hospital setting did you have a mentor?
11. Does your organization have a formal mentoring program?
12. Did you chose your mentor or were you a part of a formal mentoring program?
13. Was your mentor of the same gender, race, and organizational level?
14. Do you believe that mentoring provides the tools necessary for African-

Americans to advance in their careers? Why?

15. Did your mentor provide you with the opportunity to interact and network with upper-level management?
16. How long did it take for you to get to your current position?
17. What factor or factors do you think contributed to your career success?
18. Based on your educational achievement, tenure, and professional experience, do you believe that you have been given the opportunity for advancement in your career?

Mentor: An experienced, influential member of an organization who provides career guidance and psychosocial support to a less experienced organizational member . . . . Mentors serve as role models and provide protégés with their time, support, direction and feedback regarding career plans, actions and interpersonal development (Fagenson & Amendola 1993, p. 58)

APPENDIX E: PILOT STUDY INTERVIEW QUESTIONNAIRE

Participant Number

Age

Position

Professional Degree

Number of beds in the organization

Size of department and number of direct reports if any

1. How long have you been employed in healthcare? How long have you worked for your current organization?
2. Are you satisfied with your current job?
3. Do you feel that you have achieved your career goals?
4. What is the highest level of management in the organization that you believe you will achieve?
5. Please explain why.
6. Were you mentored at any time during your career?
7. Please give your definition of mentoring.
8. Describe the role of your mentor.
9. At what point in your career did you have your first interaction with a mentor?
10. For what period during your professional career in a hospital setting did you have a mentor?
11. Does your organization have a formal mentoring program?
12. Who determined that you would be involved in a mentoring relationship?
13. Was your mentor of the same gender, race, and/or organizational level?

14. Do you believe that mentoring is important in career advancement for African Americans? Why or why not?
15. Was your mentor instrumental in providing you with the necessary exposure to key decision makers in your organization?
16. At the commencement of your mentorship, do you believe that your mentor was instrumental in providing you with the tools necessary for your next level of management?
17. Was the interaction and networking with upper level management instrumental in the success of your career?
18. How long did it take for you to get to your current position? Describe your career path.
19. What factor do you think contributed to your career success?
20. Based on your educational achievement, tenure, and professional experience, do you believe that you have been given the opportunity for advancement in your career?
21. How successful do you feel you have been in achieving your career goals?

Mentor: someone who serves as an advisor or practical teacher with whom you intimately communicate about issues of a professional nature. And if you're fortunate, this may be a person you're already associated with, such as an instructor/practitioner you currently know or had a good connection with in the past. She or he possesses greater insight and more extensive experience in areas you want to strengthen (McCluskey, 2005, p. 3).

APPENDIX F: RESULTS TABLES

Table 1

Summary of Organizational Characteristics of the Sample

Participant Number	Number of Beds in the Organization	Size of Department	Number of Direct Reports
1		40,000 visits annually	1
8	350	22 employees	3
2	800	30 employees	30
3	Over 1500		65
4		40,000 visits annually	16
5	1100		9
6	1500		5
7	1500	235	7
9	40	239 employees, 28,000 patients per year	11
10	239	52 employees	52
11	900	30 employees	3
12	964	325 employees	9
13	1000	18 employees	15
14		30 attending physicians	9
15	Over 300	60 employees	15
16	3300	8 employees	7
17	1600	6 employees	5

Table 1 (*Continued*)

19	300	14 emergency department beds	45
20	Over 300	20 employees	5
21	Over 1500	350 employees, 100,000 visits annually	10
22	Over 1400	1000 beds	0

Table 2

Summary of Demographic Characteristics of the Sample

Participant Number	Mentor Status	Age	Education
1	No	54	B.S. in Pharmacy
8	No	46	Doctor of Pharmacy
2	Yes	46	B.A. in Pharmacy
3	Yes	41	Doctor of Pharmacy
4	Yes	60	B.S. in Nursing, M.S. in another field
5	Yes	62	Doctor of Pharmacy
6	Yes	55	Master's in Nursing
7	Yes	56	Doctor of Pharmacy
9	Yes	59	Registered Nurse
10	Yes	51	Doctor of Pharmacy
11	Yes	42	Master's in Business Administration
12	Yes	46	Doctor of Pharmacy
13	Yes	51	Doctor of Medicine
14	Yes	41	Doctor of Medicine
15	Yes	44	Doctor of Medicine
16	Yes	Under 50	Master's in Business Administration

Participant Number	Mentor Status	Age	Education
17	Yes	55	Doctor of Medicine
19	Yes	49	Nurse Practitioner
20	Yes	49	Master's in Social Work
21	Yes	50	Master's in Nursing
22	Yes	53	Master's in Health Administration

Table 3

Summary of Employment Characteristics of the Sample

Participant Number	Position	Years Working in Healthcare	Years with the Organization
1	Pharmacy Supervisor	28	11
8	Director of Pharmacy	10	0
2	Pharmacy Operations Coordinator	25	3
3	Director of Ambulatory Pharmacy	18	15
4	Director of Patient Services		
5	Director of Pharmacy	33	27
6	Associate Director of Patient Care Services	34	28
7	Director of Pharmacy Practice Residency Program and Coordinator of Education and Training	33	
9	Chief Executive Officer	38	3
10	Director of Pharmacy	30	2
11	Director of Pharmacy	22	5

Table 3 (*Continued*)

12	Director of Pharmacy	25	21
13	Medical Director	23	20
14	Assistant Professor of Clinical Obstetrics and Gynecology, Director of Obstetrics and Gynecology	26	13
15	Director of Pediatric Emergency Medicine and Medical Director of the Pediatric Emergency Department.	15	12
16	Director of Organizational Development?	4	1
17	Professor of Medicine and Director of Hepatology	25	25
19	Nurse Manager of Pediatric Emergency Dept.	27	14
20	Director of Mental Health Center and Director of Ambulatory Care	20	5

Table 3 (*Continued*)

21	Director of Patient Care Services for the Emergency Department	26	22
22	Provisional Service Line Director for Cardiovascular Services	23	21

Table 4

Professional Goals and Job Satisfaction

Participant Number	Expected Highest Level of Organizational Management	Why is That the Highest Expected Level (and Not Something Higher)?	Has Achieved Career Goals	Job Satisfaction
1	Chief Executive Officer of the hospital	"Personal choices . . . for the balance, for my personal life and . . . professional life"	"At this point yes, but I'm still not at the top yet but it's progressing nicely. I'm satisfied with my progress"	Satisfied
8	"Site administrator"	"[need to] build up some more time and get to understand the bureaucracy and the policies within the organization"	"career goals expand far beyond this"	Satisfied
2	Current position	"too much job responsibility"	"I wouldn't say I've achieved my career goals but I have reached a fairly high point"	Very satisfied

Participant Number	Expected Highest Level of Organizational Management	Why is That the Highest Expected Level (and Not Something Higher)?	Has Achieved Career Goals	Job Satisfaction
3	Vice President	"Being a CEO would be too demanding"	No	Satisfied
4	Current position	"Because I am retiring in August"	Yes	Satisfied
5	Current position	"that's all I aspire for"	"Partially"	Satisfied
6	Director	"That's the only level I'm interested in achieving"	"Not yet"	"Pretty satisfied"
7	Director of Pharmacy	"I may reach the target [retirement] age before I can achieve that"	"there are some that I feel that I have not achieved yet"	"80% satis-faction"
9	Current position	Already CEO	"Definitely"	"Yes and no"
10	Current position	"This is the highest level in Pharmacy unless it's going to be a director position"	"I think I have achieved most, but I still have a lot of goals"	Very satisfied

Participant Number	Expected Highest Level of Organizational Management	Why is That the Highest Expected Level (and Not Something Higher)?	Has Achieved Career Goals	Job Satisfaction
11	Current position	"I want to be in a career where I have more time for my family"	No, because "my career goals have changed over the course of the years"	Satisfied
12	Vice President	Wants a position this high due to "performance as a leader"	Yes	Satisfied
13	Current position	"I don't like politics"	Yes	Un-satisfied
14	Current position	"my desire is for flexibility to allow for family time"	"Not all of them"	Satisfied
15	Current position	"where I am is where I can make the most impact"	"not yet"	Satisfied

Participant Number	Expected Highest Level of Organizational Management	Why is That the Highest Expected Level (and Not Something Higher)?	Has Achieved Career Goals	Job Satisfaction
16	Vice president	"Because I don't plan to be working for anyone long enough for [a higher position] to occur"	Yes	Satisfied
17	Department Chief	"There's no additional incentive to go any higher" and "I don't think they're going to give someone Black a . . . Chairmanship of a Department"	Yes	Satisfied
19	Director of Pediatric Services	"I don't think that getting a senior position would be within the remaining time that I plan to be working"	Yes	Very satisfied
20	Vice President	"Because that's the next step from the position which I'm in"	Not yet	Satisfied

Participant Number	Expected Highest Level of Organizational Management	Why is That the Highest Expected Level (and Not Something Higher)?	Has Achieved Career Goals	Job Satisfaction
21	Current position	"in our organizational structure this . . . is the highest level"	"There's still more to attain but I'm . . . on target"	Satisfied
22	Vice President or a Senior Vice President	Wants to obtain this high level "Because I'm very competent"	"as I mature . . . my goals continue to evolve so I'm still achieving goals"	Satisfied

Table 5

Explicit Definitions of Mentoring

Participant Number	Definition
1	When "one who has achieved professional status [helps] you get where you want to go . . . they can give you ins and outs of certain behavior patterns, who to see, what to say, what to do, what's expected of you, such that you will achieve your goals"
8	When "you take someone under your wing . . . provide them with leadership . . . a big brother, a father, a teacher, a counselor, coach . . . and you guide that person's career and help them to achieve their best"
2	"When someone takes you under their wings and show you . . . things that you can do"
3	Someone "you can talk to about where you are and they can assist you in making the right decisions . . . they can give you their experience and can help you to shape a path"
4	"Someone in the organization that will take you and guide you and help you to learn your job so that you can be better at what you do. Someone who will help you along the way, who serves as a resource"

Participant Number	Definition
5	A mentor is "someone with professional experience that you are trying to acquire that's willing to give of himself"
6	"Mentoring . . . is taking someone under your wing and helping to guide them and grow professionally . . . to me it's a relationship that's established in a deliberate manner"
7	"Someone who can have an impact on a person either as a role model or in some way as a facilitator/advisor. Mentoring to me is very personal. Some people look at it as possibly a way to just have someone you can call upon but in order to be effective you have to be able to expose your weaknesses and your strengths as well"
9	"Someone who helps you set goals and objectives, helps you get there in reaching those goals and objectives; helps you tell you what the pitfalls are, what you need to do and is there just to guide you along the way"
10	"Mentoring means somebody . . . who shows you the ropes, showing you what to do, when and how . . . be an example, basically"

Participant Number	Definition
11	"Mentoring for me was teaching professionalism and how to act accordingly; teaching diplomacy and tact, identifying my failures and providing suggestions on how to succeed, listening, supporting and trusting decisions even though they were risky; allowing me to make my mistakes and dealing with the consequences . . . managing my productivity and . . . pointing out opportunities to succeed"
12	"Mentoring is to have someone in a leadership position that has experience in a particular area where you'd like to go or that you think that you would like to achieve"
13	"Someone who helps . . . guides you and gives you different ways to solve a problem"
14	"Someone who basically took me under their wings and made sure that I understood career choices, position choices, insurance choices, the ins and outs of business; somebody who really . . . had my best interest at heart when it came to the practice of medicine but also the business of medicine"
15	"A mentor is someone who can advice you on your career and sometimes on your personal [and] professional [lives] . . . sort of how they relate to each other at any given point in your career."

Participant Number	Definition
16	"An experienced individual who can share insight and provide specific guidance on how to achieve goals and in the process how to avoid de-railers"
17	"Mentoring would be someone who is a younger person who is being . . . not pushed but . . . prepared to take on another position, a higher position"
19	"Mentoring is teaching someone the ropes, helping them to navigate their professional field so that they too can be successful in whatever area that they chose to go . . . helping someone to network . . . give them the information they need to be better able to function at their job"
20	"Mentoring is being . . . nurtured by other women at an executive level to be able to find direction in my career"
21	"Someone that had attained certain things that I was aspiring to. I was able to go and talk to them about how did they do it, what can I do to improve my position"
22	"Someone who provides a listening ear and serves as a sounding board for my ideas my thoughts, any issues or problems . . . that person provides you with some guidance from their experience base"

Table 6

Themes Derived from the Explicit Definitions of Mentoring

Participant Number	Has Professional Experience	A Good Listener	Establishes a Personal Relationship	Sets an Example/ Serves as a Role Model	Brings Out Your Best/Achieve Goals
1	Yes				Yes
8			Yes		Yes
2			Yes		Yes
3	Yes	Yes			
4					Yes
5	Yes			Yes	
6			Yes		
7		Yes	Yes	Yes	
9					Yes
10				Yes	
11		Yes			
12	Yes			Yes	Yes
13					
14			Yes		
15			Yes		
16	Yes				Yes
17	Yes				
19					Yes

Participant Number	Has Professional Experience	A Good Listener	Establishes a Personal Relationship	Sets an Example/ Serves as a Role Model	Brings Out Your Best/Achieve Goals
20					
21	Yes	Yes		Yes	Yes
22	Yes	Yes			
Total Mentions	8 (38.1%)	5 (23.8%)	6 (28.6%)	5 (23.8%)	9 (42.9%)

Table 7

Role of Respondents Personal Mentor

Participant Number	Personal Mentor Role
2	"She gave me professional guidance . . . stepping outside the box of just being a pharmacist allowed me to do a lot of other things and take on more projects and extend outside of that role, just being a pharmacist"
3	"Helped to really get serious about my career direction, what I was doing, what choices I needed to make in order to get to that point that I was trying to reach and helped me make decisions . . . talked me through that stage . . . gave me insight into the policies of the organization and helped me to maneuver in making sure that some of the decisions that I made were not emotional"
4	"helped me to learn my job and answered questions for me when I needed help"
5	"When I had problems, for instance professional problems, I could call and get their opinion and either implement it or tweak it, one way or the other"
6	"My supervisor, my director . . . I guess deliberatively I've learned from her"

Participant Number	Personal Mentor Role
7	"My mentor was one who had the ability to force me to think about things . . . I felt that my mentor was like a father, he was like family and it gave me a very strong emotional feeling knowing that he was present and that he was always there for me . . . great mentoring it really does become a very personal matter . . . when my mentor decided to leave me I felt the sadness of someone dying"
9	"Helped me to set goals that were sometimes in my mind not achievable, but she . . . had a vision for me, and put that out there for me to achieve, and steered me in the direction of achieving that goal"
10	"For me mentoring has been great because you get into a new system and . . . even though you're probably trained in the area the organization has its own ways of doing business or politics and by being mentored you grab on to these policies quicker than usual. Mentoring to me, especially now working in a hospital environment is [going to] help me to know the rules and avoid disciplinary action within that framework"
11	"She's not a micro manager . . . she allows me to go to the field but keeps a very careful eye on me. when it comes to professionalism, I lacked it in some ways"
12	"Primarily for career guidance"

Participant Number	Personal Mentor Role
13	"It wasn't a formal mentorship . . . but he gave me direction and helped me to explore what other areas was I interested in, and learn from that interaction"
14	"Helped me understand the potential that I had, when I was young, and to understand the value of education . . . once I was headed in the medical field then my professional mentors really helped me to understand what I valued and then to seek those sorts of things in my career choices"
15	"her role is to meet with me and advice me on grant writing and assistance with funding and contacts and research critique and ideas"
16	"They were senior executives . . . in one case they were in my division and in another it was a totally different area of responsibility, but all senior levels, senior VPs"
17	"The role of my mentor was to encourage me to independently develop protocols, clinical trials and to publish chapters, book chapters and things of that sort"

Participant Number	Personal Mentor Role
19	"I have strong issues with employee management, and she will help me on a monthly or weekly basis depending on how often we are able to meet on how best to handle the specific situation . . . she is very specific . . . she gives me the nuts and bolts to managing the situation . . . she looks at where I am and she is very upfront, very honest . . . to the core . . . she kind of pulls the reign in to make sure . . . help me do what I need to do for guidance"
20	"They helped to keep me calm . . . focused"
21	"Just there to help me plan my career path . . . different ways that I could go about achieving that"
22	"She was like my barometer . . . she would listen to me confidentially so if I had an issue with a person or an organization or direction or strategy she would sort of put things in perspective for me . . . trying to put things in perspective"

Table 8

Importance of Mentors for African Americans to Advance in Their Careers

Participant Number	General Statement of Importance	Mentor Was Same Gender and Race	Importance of Mentors

Participant Number	General Statement of Importance	Mentor Was Same Gender and Race	Importance of Mentors
1	Very important	NA	"Most definitely. If there was a structured mentorship or mentor program of which these aspiring (especially the young kids coming in) can tap into they would have knowledge and camaraderie . . . we don't have that . . . that would be a God send"
8	Important	NA	"If I can find a mentor, yes it does"
2	Important	Same gender but not race	"Yes, I think it does because it opens up doors that sometimes are not there, and it gives you an opportunity to sometimes see things that you don't necessarily see . . . because if the person that is over you is really open and accepting you will get that opportunity"

Participant Number	General Statement of Importance	Mentor Was Same Gender and Race	Importance of Mentors
3	Very important	Same gender and race	"I wouldn't limit it only to African Americans but I think that mentoring is a good tool for any individual, whatever career track, so, and the reason I say that is that as you evolve in your professional career, there are things that will happen that you have no experience how to handle. It allows you a tool to relieve some of the stress. I do feel mentoring provides the necessary tool"
4	Very important	Different gender but same race	"Yes I believe that African Americans need a mentor to help them to get to t he next level of management. They need someone to help them to get into the inner circle. There are politics and cliques and without someone to take them and help them along the way, they may become discouraged and lost along the way"

Participant Number	General Statement of Importance	Mentor Was Same Gender and Race	Importance of Mentors
5	Very important	Different gender but same race	"I do believe that it is an excellent tool . . . it's nothing new and most folk have been doing this with each other for years. The majority race has been doing this for years grooming someone to either take their place or go out and do whatever they are doing. The reason why I believe it works is because it helps you get to a higher point or knowledge much quicker than having to gain all the experiences yourself"

Participant Number	General Statement of Importance	Mentor Was Same Gender and Race	Importance of Mentors
6	Very important	-	"Absolutely . . . the problem is many times African Americans, the literature shows anyway, women in minorities tend to get the least amount of mentoring, the least amount of feedback, and so its [going to] be very important for us because many of us do not have family members and counterparts that are at higher levels because historically we haven't achieved those positions, so for us to learn and grow we've got to have someone to show us the way"

Participant Number	General Statement of Importance	Mentor Was Same Gender and Race	Importance of Mentors
7	Important	Same gender and race	"I believe that mentoring provides the tools necessary . . . not to say that's it's impossible [without mentoring] but it becomes much better for you to have someone that you can call upon that can help you to give you those strengths you need to get to where you want to go . . . I think that is very important that you have a mentor, especially when you're trying to reach a high level. Often times it is a very lonely position to be in when you don't have someone that you can turn to as a mentor"
9	Important	Different gender and race	"If it's a formal program yes, and there are so many things that you don't know so mentoring would surely help you if you had someone to guide you . . . because it does take a lot of work, if you're going to do it right"

Participant Number	General Statement of Importance	Mentor Was Same Gender and Race	Importance of Mentors
10	Very important	Different gender but same race	"For me mentoring has been great because you get into a new system . . . even though you're probably trained in the area the organization has its own ways of doing business or politics and by being mentored you grab on to these policies quicker than usual . . . mentoring to me, especially now working in a hospital environment help[s] me to know the rules and avoid disciplinary action within that framework"
11	Very important	Same gender but different race	"The level of knowledge I had, there was no way I would have made it, I was too rough . . . it took someone else to show me I was rough . . . I think it happens to a lot of us, a lot of African Americans now . . . we have the ability to do the work and do it well, but it's what comes with it that we don't have"

Participant Number	General Statement of Importance	Mentor Was Same Gender and Race	Importance of Mentors
12	Potentially important	Different gender and race	"I think the process, depending on who the person is, yes, would give you an opportunity to prepare you for other types of positions but there are a lot of factors that actually determine whether that is effective or not . . . It has to be the right person, it's the time, you know it may not occur at the time when you expect it to occur and it also determines"
13	Potentially important	-	"If you have someone who is going to encourage you and guide you in your career, yes"

Participant Number	General Statement of Importance	Mentor Was Same Gender and Race	Importance of Mentors
14	Very important	Same gender but different race	"Absolutely . . . for those of us who have had mentors . . . it has been very beneficial . . . there definitely are some inherent things in the system that are not necessarily to our advantage, that we are not taught, per se, but are things that you find out the hard way, so I think having a mentor absolutely was helpful"

Participant Number	General Statement of Importance	Mentor Was Same Gender and Race	Importance of Mentors
15	Potentially important	Same gender but different race	"Yes and no . . . I think for the academic parts of it some yes, I'd say the ones who have paved or have sort of achieved success in a certain area, like say research for instance . . . they can help guide you in the sort of black and white of it, you know the objective pieces of it . . . I think though that sometimes the other portions, the more personal part in where your home and family life impact on your career sometimes not so much, because there are some different cultural values, and even though my mentor is of the same gender she's of a different generation and had a different sort of cultural experience than I had . . . so I think for a total of a positive mentoring experience, I think of all the professional, personal, you can't really separate them, especially if you are a female African American…it provides some of the academic tools, but it's not 100% great"

Participant Number	General Statement of Importance	Mentor Was Same Gender and Race	Importance of Mentors
16	Very important	Different gender and race	"I think it's definitely helpful . . . I don't know that it's the end all, but . . . you're much more likely to achieve your goals of growing in an organization with the help of a mentor . . . I think that it's also helpful if that mentor is passionate about helping others"
17	Very important	Same gender but different race	"Because they need direction . . . they need direction; they need to learn how to climb the ladder, what they have to do . . . for example, publications, clinical trials, to be encouraged into that"

Participant Number	General Statement of Importance	Mentor Was Same Gender and Race	Importance of Mentors
19	Potentially important	Same gender but different race	"Yes [but] it depends on your mentor . . . if the mentor is really true and wants to see you grow, they will provide you with the tools to help you to grow . . . if it's a mentor who is just in the program just because their company offers it and they are just going to go through the ropes of this and that's it, then you won't really learn, you won't benefit from it . . . based on the ones that I've been through at this system, and been exposed to at the previous systems that I worked with, yes, you can definitely grow"
20	Important	Same gender and race	"Yes, I do believe so because there are very few [of] us and we need to know that the plight that we're having, or the concerns or the frustrations are just natural for who we are and where we are going"

Participant Number	General Statement of Importance	Mentor Was Same Gender and Race	Importance of Mentors
21	Very important	Same gender but different race	"I believe it helps . . . sometimes we don't know the steps to take, the road to take . . . a number of going to professional careers, especially to the levels that we have achieved might have had parents who finished high school but they didn't go to college, or some had parents who never even went to high school . . . so having a mentor in the work environment helps us to navigate a lot of the nuances of the professional world that we probably would not be able to just go home and talk to our mom about . . . therefore, I think a mentor is very helpful, especially to African Americans"

Participant Number	General Statement of Importance	Mentor Was Same Gender and Race	Importance of Mentors
22	Very important	Same gender and race	"Absolutely . . . because it gives us a little bit more of an inside track that we may not have had exposure to . . . many of us, not all of us, but many of us don't come from families who are in corporate America at high levels . . . so it gives us really an exposure to someone who is a part of the organization and we learn the various levels and the cultural things that are going on in the organization and its just like having your foot in the door"

APPENDIX G: PERMISSION TO USE PREMISES

UNIVERSITY OF PHOENIX

INFORMED CONSENT: PERMISSION TO USE PREMISES, NAME, AND/OR SUBJECTS

(Facility, Organization, University, Institution, or Association)

Black Nurses Association
Name of Facility, Organization, University, Institution, or Association

I hereby authorize Deon Wolliston, student of University of Phoenix, to use the premises, name and/or subjects requested to conduct a study entitled African-American Decision-Makers in Healthcare:Exploring the impact of mentoring on professional advancement.

Signature　　　　　　　　Date: 4,9,07

President
Title

Black Nurses Association
Name of Facility

UNIVERSITY OF PHOENIX

INFORMED CONSENT: PERMISSION TO USE PREMISES, NAME, AND/OR SUBJECTS

(Facility, Organization, University, Institution, or Association)

Association of Black Health-Systems Pharmacist
Name of Facility, Organization, University, Institution, or Association

I hereby authorize Deon Wolliston, student of University of Phoenix, to use the premises, name and/or subjects requested to conduct a study entitled African-American Decision-Makers in Healthcare:Exploring the impact of mentoring on professional advancement.

John E. Clark
Signature

4/5/07
Date

President, ABHP
Title

Association of Black Health-Systems Pharmacists
Name of Facility

UNIVERSITY OF PHOENIX

INFORMED CONSENT: PERMISSION TO USE PREMISES, NAME, AND/OR SUBJECTS

(Facility, Organization, University, Institution, or Association)

Jackson Memorial Health System
Name of Facility, Organization, University, Institution, or Association

I hereby authorize Deon Wolliston, student of University of Phoenix, to use the premises, name and/or subjects requested to conduct a study entitled African-American Decision-Makers in Healthcare:Exploring the impact of mentoring on professional advancement.

Signature | Date

Director of Compliance
Title

Jackson Memorial Health System
Name of Facility

UNIVERSITY OF PHOENIX

INFORMED CONSENT: PERMISSION TO USE PREMISES, NAME, AND/OR SUBJECTS

(Facility, Organization, University, Institution, or Association)

Tallahassee Memorial HealthCare, Inc.
Name of Facility, Organization, University, Institution, or Association

I hereby authorize Deon Wolliston, student of University of Phoenix, to use the premises, name and/or subjects requested to conduct a study entitled African-American Decision-Makers in Healthcare:Exploring the impact of mentoring on professional advancement.

G. Mark O'Bryant
Signature

04/26/07
Date

President/CEO
Title

Tallahassee Memorial HealthCare, Inc.
Name of Facility

TMH IRB # 2007-09

Prinicpal Investigator: Deon Wolliston, MSN, ARNP

Study Title: African-American Decision Makers in HealthCare: Exploring the Impact of Mentoring on Professional Advancement

Address: 17903 SW 35th Court, Miramar, Florida 33029

Phone #: (H) 954-432-7785 (C) 954-895-2033 E-mail: deonlw@bellsouth.net

EXPEDITED REVIEW CHECKLIST

Tallahassee Memorial HealthCare (TMH) – Institutional Review Board (IRB)

A PROJECT IS ELIGIBLE FOR EXPEDITED REVIEW IF:

- The project passes certain initial eligibility tests, and
- All of the project's human subject research falls within one or more of the expedited review categories defined by government regulations.

If you think your project qualifies, submit this checklist with a submission letter, protocol, an Informed Consent Form (if applicable) and a completed *APPLICATION FOR IRB WAIVER OF HIPAA PRIVACY AUTHORIZATION* (obtain form from TMH Office of Research/IRB 850-431-5676).

ELIGIBILITY TESTS

Preliminary Questions:

YES	NO	Does your project involve:
☐	☒	Clinical studies of medical devices, procedures, treatments, or drugs?
☐	☒	Pregnant women, fetuses, neonates, or human in vitro fertilization?
☐	☒	Prisoners?

If you answered YES to any of these questions, your project is NOT eligible for expedited review by the TMH IRB. If you answered NO, continue

Test I : Minimal Risk

Does any part of your project present more than minimal risk to human subjects?

Minimal Risk means that the probability and magnitude of harm or discomfort anticipated in the research are not greater in and of themselves than those ordinarily encountered in daily life or during the performance of routine physical or psychological examinations or tests. ☐YES ☒NO

If you answered... NO.... Your project passes Test I
YES... Your project fails Test I, and it not eligible for expedited review.

MH IRB #)C

Test II: Identity Risks & Protections

(a) Could identification of the subjects and/or their responses reasonably place them at risk of criminal or c il liability or be damaging to the subjects financial standing, employability, insurability, reputation, or be stigmatizing? ☐YES ☒NO

(b) Will reasonable and appropriate protect ons be implemented so that risks related to invasion of priv and breach of confidentiality are no greater han minimal? ☒YES ☐NO

If you answere NO tc
YES or t pas: II

YES to (a) AND
NO to (b) our projec ails Test II, and not eligibl for expedited review.

est III: Classified Research

Does your project involve classified human subjects research? ☐YES ☒NO

If you answered... NO...... Your project passes Test III
YES..... Your project fails Test III, and is not eligible for expedited review.

est IV: Qualification for Expedited Review

Does all the human subject research in your project fall into one or more of review categories? (Refer to the attached category and eligibility descriptions)

☒YES Cat# 6 — Your project passes T t IV and ible for expedited view

☐NO — Your project requires full-board IRB review. Complete a *Checklist For ew Stud* Obtain this checklist from the TMH Medical Staff Office 850/431-5122

If your study passed ests I, III ND IV he ligibility tests Expedited Review.

IRB USE ONLY

I certify that I have reviewed all documentation for this study and it is approved for Expedited Review.

Larry C. Deeb, M.D., Chair/IRB — *Date*